Artists as Professors

University of Illinois Press *Urbana Chicago London*

ARTISTS AS PROFESSORS

Conversations with
Musicians, Painters, Sculptors

Morris Risenhoover and Robert T. Blackburn

Library of Congress Cataloging in Publication Data

Risenhoover, Morris, 1940–
  Artists as professors.

  Bibliography: p.
  1. Artists as teachers. 2. Artists—United States—
Interviews. 3. Art—Study and teaching (Higher)—
United States. 4. College teachers as artists.
I. Blackburn, Robert T., joint author. II. Title.
NX304.R57   700'.92'2   75-38681
ISBN 0-252-00574-0

Institutions and genius are in the nature
of things antithetical, and if a man of genius
is found living contentedly in the university,
it is peculiarly creditable to both.

Charles Cooley

Contents

Preface

Our subject is the artist as professor. At issue is whether the university milieu provides a hospitable environment for an artist's professional activities—as artist as well as teacher.

What happens when outstanding artists join a faculty? Is their creativity altered? How effective are they as teachers? Are there satisfactions which compensate for the stresses and constraints most people believe to be inevitable when creative individuals are housed in bureaucratic organizations?

We talked with artist-teachers about these issues. Several factors suggested we confine our investigation to musicians and to painters and others working in the visual arts. While we were equally curious about actors, dancers, and writers, we wanted to interview individuals who already enjoy full faculty status in fields where university roots go deeper.

Poets and novelists visit campuses, but with few exceptions have not become professors in departments of English, which traditionally have dealt with criticism rather than artistic creation. Distinguished actors and directors have not joined academic communities, where serious theater is still often treated as an extracurricular activity. Dance, if it appears at all, often exists as a course in the women's physical education department. There are exceptions to this pattern—a department of creative writing or a school of the arts—but the instances are both rare and recent, albeit increasing. For the moment, musicians and practitioners in the visual arts are the only ones in appreciable numbers to have found permanent professorships in universities. Hence our decision to restrict the investigation to persons in these two categories.

There is a geographical restriction in addition to disciplinary ones. Artists meeting the highest professional criteria are not randomly distributed across the country. Rather, they are heavily concentrated in leading universities in the East, Northeast, and Midwest. (Expenses partially limited our sample. We could not travel everywhere we wished—to the West Coast, for example—to interview individuals meeting the criteria.)

Finally, most of our interviewees are males. We do not know how much this imbalance is a consequence of an uneven sex distribution within the arts and to what degree it reflects the employment practices of universities. Most likely, a combination of both exists. We have noted the hiring of more distinguished female artists as professors since our interviews were held.

In all, forty-three artists consented to interviews in their studios or homes. They were selected on the basis of distinguished artistic achievement and recognition. The tape-recorded sessions lasted from one to three hours. Nineteen transcribed interviews then were chosen to guarantee artistic diversity—composers, performers, painters, sculptors—and to give range and scope of responses. The transcriptions have been edited by us to transmit the general truths discovered in a larger study.

A historical sketch precedes the interviews. This essay examines the development of schooling in the arts and sets the context for the conversations with the artists. A concluding essay examines the contributions artist-professors are making to universities. It also suggests how academic life can be made even richer than it now is for the long-time resident academics as well as for the newly arrived artist-professors.

We are much indebted to our respondents for their time and for permission to print our interviews with them.

Artists as Professors

Art, Artists, and Universities

The arts have flourished on college campuses, especially since World War II. Handsome new arts centers decorate quadrangles and outstanding artists have migrated to universities.

As a varied scope of campus arts programs emerges, the contemporary university has partially displaced or absorbed long-standing cultural institutions—opera companies, symphonic and choral organizations, conservatories of music, and academies of art. University involvement in the arts has been an important factor in the much-signaled decentralization of cultural life in the United States. Whereas cities such as New York, Chicago, San Francisco (and perhaps a half-dozen more) were *the* centers of rich and varied artistic activity, now a number of cities, tiny by comparison, boast a flourishing artistic milieu.

We must understand the evolution of this relationship between the arts and the university in order to appreciate fully the remarks of the interviewed artists. After all, the generation before them worked outside universities and even now some artist-professors question the legitimacy of their new home. Furthermore, not all of the arts are in full bloom in institutions of higher learning.

We need to comprehend the causes which produced today's artistic organization and processes in our colleges for other reasons as well. Recognizing factors which have shaped current arrangements between the arts and universities gives a basis for prognosticating tomorrow. The following overview of art, artists, and universities offers the needed perspective.

INSTITUTIONAL GROWTH AND DEVELOPMENT

Colonial American colleges adopted the English model of higher education. A fixed, classical curriculum prepared young

3

gentlemen for society's leadership positions—for the ministry, law, and medicine. If these graduates were to be "cultured" men, their formal study took little account of the arts. Like learning French, familiarity with music and painting were thought of as "accomplishments," harmless enough in themselves but definitely to be pursued outside academe.

After personal and national survival had been assured and as interest in the arts grew in this country, private proprietary teaching institutions for artists were established. Certainly painters taught in ateliers, and musicians taught in studios and homes. But by the 1880s most principal cities also had conservatories of music and schools of art. These were intended to be professional, post-secondary institutions but most often they were of far less than professional quality. American students who wished to seriously pursue studies in the arts had to go to Europe for the finishing touches to their preparation. (They did not, however, attend universities, for the European educational system, like the early American one, excluded artistic activity from its curriculum.)

Concurrent with the flourishing of separate teaching institutions devoted to the arts, a few colleges began to recognize the benefits of offering instruction in the arts. Such colleges were rarely in the East (where to this day professional work in the arts is less prevalent than elsewhere) and were usually girls' schools (where education in music and the visual arts was very popular and hence profitable for the college). The quality of the instruction was generally lower than that obtainable in the private conservatories and schools of art. The day when distinguished artists would take posts in colleges and universities was still some time away.

As the country expanded westward, however, public universities were founded, and by 1850 a new tradition was set. State and land-grant universities were especially receptive to expanding professional programs as well as to the idea of being of service to the public at large. Public universities viewed themselves as capstones of the educational system, and it was in their atmosphere of service, accommodation, and openness to new ideas that the highest caliber of professional education began to be included in university programs. Earliest entries were law and medicine. Then an emphasis on science, the addition of schools of education and business, and, finally, a serious commitment to the arts emerged in public universities.

To suppose the intrusion of the arts was accomplished without a murmur of dissent from the academy would be to err. It should be recalled that early in the nineteenth century both Harvard and Yale had to establish separate scientific schools when experimenters wanted to bring the actual practice of scientific manipulations and research into the university. A somewhat similar pattern occurred with the arts a hundred years later. Musicology, art history, and the study of drama and poetry as literature (as well as literary criticism, of course) long had been honored as eminently respectable academic disciplines. But when it later was asserted that the analysis of art ought to hold no more sacrosanct position in the academy than the actual creation and realization through performance of such works, critics suggested that the university was opting to teach mere technique and craftsmanship, just as the criticisms had raged concerning the practice of science a century before. Such objections, however, eventually were overridden since they were essentially antithetical to the evolutionary trend the American university was taking. Accretion and expansion had become the accepted practice in higher education. By now the university has come to its position of wide acceptance as the logical home for the arts in this country.

While large, complex universities with a variety of professional schools were developing, other events converged to hasten the decline of the private conservatories and schools of art. The Great Depression of the 1930s resulted in the collapse of a large proportion of such enterprises. For those which survived, the 1940s and '50s brought new economic and social pressures. Expenses for operations leaped. Accreditation agencies and influential professional associations required curricular scope and quality unattainable by many. The stronger institutions affiliated with colleges and universities so as to meet the social pressures for "going to college" that arose from students and their families. The weaker simply closed.[1]

Other social forces accelerated the movement of instruction in the arts to college campuses. For example, as universal secondary education became a reality in this century, the need for high school teachers in the arts intensified. The demand was especially acute in music. Bands not only provided Saturday night concerts in village squares, they also aroused the same kind of community pride that a winning athletic team did. River City had to have qualified instructors if seventy-six trombones were to play in unison. And so certified bachelor degrees in music education—not performance—swelled enrollments at the collegiate level.

The visual arts lagged behind music in their higher education development. American society has not accepted painters as it has pianists. A Bohemian life-style may be romantic but it flaunts the Protestant work ethic. Also, the vocational payoff is even less clear for the artist than for the musician. In addition, the arts apparently possess a sexual taint. Either sex may blow horns or pluck strings, but only female adolescents can dabble in clay and watercolors and weaving. Peers and parents challenge the masculinity of the teenager who prefers dirtying himself with oils rather than the grease of an automobile motor or the mud of the gridiron.[2] Hence high school instruction in the

1. Another response some art schools made was to add a liberal arts faculty. They became specialized undergraduate institutions, much like technological institutes in the engineering sciences. Yet for many academies the action was too late and inadequate.

2. Dance, theater, and writing poetry have even less acceptance in American culture. Furthermore, as semi-legitimate residents in already existing units (theater in speech departments, for example), there are actually more obstacles in the way of their flourishing and expanding then when a new unit is formed for the expressed purposes of growing and developing.

As for the future of these arts in universities, fewer certainties exist. Besides not being in demand as teachers in the elementary and secondary schools, novelists, for example, are classified as luxuries and are bound to suffer with eco-

arts has never become as systematized or as extensive as it has in music and consequently departments of art remain less developed than schools of music. However, the spread of popular higher education in this country has greatly strengthened the visual arts areas. While parents will not support their children for four years of living in North Beach, they will finance them to a baccalaureate in art at San Francisco State. The latter is legitimate. It certifies its product with a credential and meets socially acceptable criteria. Institutionalized higher education is, after all, an American "good." Moreover, the division of labor and resulting specialization made possible by forming a large organization of professionals for instruction had irresistible appeal for leaders interested in the preparation of musicians just as it earlier had for the training of lawyers.

Perhaps more than any other social force, the economic factor has led universities to accept their present role as leaders in instruction in the arts. Bluntly stated, society has defined the American university as the place where post-secondary education ought to occur, regardless of the activity or the goal. Generally speaking, few non-university organizations seeking to fulfill comparable purposes are sufficiently recognized and supported to remain viable. Universities have not resisted the opportunity to fulfill such societal expectations. But when they undertake the mission, naturally they search for completeness in program offerings and strive to ensure continued favor and support for themselves.

From the foregoing overview, then, the emergence of the American university as headquarters for high-level instruction in the arts clearly was more influenced by forces other than what students actually wanted to learn. What professional music and art students really wanted was, and still could be, available mainly in private studios and ateliers. The same might be said of medicine and law, for that matter, but appren-

nomic adversity. All the same, times are changing. If Broadway goes the way of Greenwich Village, the professional theater may follow professional artists to campuses.

ticeships in those areas declined and disappeared for many of the same reasons. Modern society runs on a division of expert labor and requires that training be legitimized.

FACULTIES

The institutionalization of the arts within universities was not immediately paralleled by a move of leading artists to the campuses. Early music and art department faculty were prin-- cipally teachers, not practitioners. In fact, as colleges and universities drew the arts more unto themselves, there began a century of uncertainty about engaging artists as faculty members.

As long as the legitimacy of appointing pianists, painters, singers, and sculptors to faculties remained unresolved, universities failed to seek and attract faculty as high in quality in those areas as they were accustomed to acquiring in the traditional disciplines. At the same time, those on concert tours and those with shows in leading galleries showed no inclination to be (in their view) constrained by place and time and committed to tasks that detracted from their creative output. Generally speaking, artists no more sought professorships than colleges sought artists.

In traditional academic disciplines, the highest standards of excellence and professional recognition were the criteria set for appointment. To be sure, even in the beginning, when universities began engaging musicians and painters for faculties, they got some very good ones. However, the criteria used in selecting them were somewhat circumscribed. A certain academic parochialism limited the search to a pool of candidates who had declared themselves in pursuit of teaching careers. Those maintaining a higher professional profile *as artists* were overlooked. Whether this practice resulted from lack of university ambition and misunderstanding of the professional qualifications desired is unclear. Equally uncertain is how serious some artists were when they proclaimed they would never take a position on a university faculty.

What was needed gradually became clearer, however. Even as early as 1916, the novel idea was advanced that "employment of the leading artist" would boost the quality of music departments in universities.[3] The first "artist-in-residence" in an American university was John Steuart Curry, appointed at the University of Wisconsin in the mid-1930s. In 1939 Curry was joined at Wisconsin by the pianist Gunnar Johansen, and Paul Sample's tenure at Dartmouth lasted from 1938 to 1962. But employing distinguished artists on campus for an extended period of time must properly be considered a post–World War II phenomenon. The trend accelerated in the 1950s and became fairly standard practice in major universities in the 1960s, by which time its rationale had become well articulated: "We need scholars in a university because students are given their best chance if they learn philosophy from philosophers, sociology from sociologists, and biology from biologists, not from historians and appreciators of philosophy, sociology, and biology, so they have their most real introduction to the arts from artists, not from historians or appreciators of the arts."[4]

The visiting artist-in-residence fails to provide the continuity needed for program development and for students desiring extensive training. If students were to become artists through university education, then permanent artist-teachers were needed in the academic community. Maybe glamor, prestige, and public relations possibilities also influenced university decisions to make a basic change in arts faculties, but it would appear that a motivating force for the presence of high-caliber

3. Rose Yont, *Status and Value of Music in Education* (Lincoln, Neb.: Woodruff Press, 1916), p. 207. The composer Edward MacDowell had been engaged by Columbia University in 1896 to be chairman of the department of music, but in 1904 he left in a huff, citing interference in departmental affairs by President Seth Low. MacDowell died two years later.

4. Russell F. W. Smith, "A Community of Artists and Scholars," *Arts in Society*, 2, no. 3 (1963), 69.

professional artists on campus had to do with students who desired to become practicing artists and not teachers.

Just why practioners are needed to prepare artists-to-be is open to debate. Artists refer to a special effect they alone can have in the education of a sculptor or cellist. It is not easy to specify exactly what comprises the special impact they believe they have. It could be the excitement of contact with famous people. Perhaps it is their example of commitment to art and to work as an artist. Maybe the drive of the artist is contagious. Or maybe the presence of the gifted artist engenders a competitiveness among students clamoring for their part of the artist's scarce teaching time. Maybe the student's desire to please an idol extracts the critical extra effort. Maybe the passing on of the small suggestion that only the accomplished artist can sense makes the difference. Whatever it is, something special happens; the extraordinary influence of artist-teachers can be traced through attestations from their students.

Establishment, growth, and development of the practice of seeking professional artists in higher educational institutions does not end the story however. By the time enthusiasm for artists as teachers in universities had attained unprecedented heights in the 1960s, there had arisen considerable popular controversy not about whether artists were fit for universities but whether universities were fit for artists. It was suggested that artists would dislike teaching and that the atmosphere in academe would prove uncongenial and even stultifying to artists' creative powers.

A few enjoy teaching as a second vocation and believe their own creativity does not suffer from it. Some enjoy teaching while believing their own work does suffer. The great majority endure teaching as a means of livelihood, suffer the fact that there may be only two or three students a year in whom they glimpse any potentialities of talent, agonize over that portion of their own creative quotient which ends in the canvases of amateurs, and yearn for the unlikely year when some agency like the Ford Foundation may permit them simply to paint. Unanimously, even including those who believe their own creativity does not suffer from teaching, the artists to whom I have talked are bitter about the fact that their students are handed to them in groups and they have no voice in screening or selecting them.[5]

That a lack of congeniality between artists and universities would be suspected is not surprising. After all, professional training in the creative and performing arts is a relatively new phenomenon in universities, and artist-teachers are correspondingly new to faculty positions. Other faculty members with their long academic lineage in the sciences and humanities expect universities to be at the forefront of concern and development within their fields. Through extensive schooling they have prepared themselves to launch an academic career. Artists, on the other hand, are more likely to have had in mind careers entirely unrelated to academic life even though they too have achieved high levels of competence through training and experience.

Also, divergence between the values and goals of artists and typical university people conceivably could run deep. A case in point is the broad scope of the university's concerns as contrasted with the often narrowly focused interests of artists. The artist deals with the particular, the subjective, and the unique object, datum, or experience as opposed to the scholar's search for the universal, the objective, and classifiable objects, data, or experiences. Further, the university's is a verbal tradition whereas artists claim their creations are not reducible to words, that analysis can destroy beauty.

Consensus regarding the possibility of a healthy relationship between creative artists and the university, then, has failed to materialize. It is thought that universities stultify, that their pure intellectualism distorts. As a bureaucracy they lack the necessary freedoms for the creative individual. So the critics say and so the artists wondered when they took their university positions.

5. W. McNeil Lowry, "The University and the Creative Arts," *Arts in Society*, 2, no. 3 (1963), 14–15.

We too believed these proclamations. In our concern for the future of the arts and in our belief that the best potential home for them was the university, we set out to learn from the leading artist-professors in the country how this unfortunate state could be improved. We thought we might uncover the key conflicts between the artist and his university and be able to propose alternative structures and processes for making the artist's environment at least minimally tolerable.

What we learned from our inquiry was that in the main the pundits were wrong. For the most part, a happy union had taken place between artists and universities. At the same time, artist-professors and traditional academics could learn from one another and improve life for both. The interviews answer questions regarding the fit between artists and universities. The closing essay analyzes how improvements could make life even richer than it now is.

Harold Altman

Harold Altman was born April 20, 1924, in New York. He studied at Cooper Union, the Art Students League, and in Paris. He has held Guggenheim, Fulbright, and National Institute of Arts and Letters awards.

His paintings have been seen in more than 150 one-man shows plus many other group exhibitions throughout Europe, Japan, and Israel, as well as the United States. His work is held in public collections of the Boston Museum of Fine Arts, the Metropolitan Museum of Art, the Museum of Modern Art, the Philadelphia Museum, and the Whitney Museum, among others.

Mr. Altman teaches at Pennsylvania State University.

Mr. Altman, how and why did you join a university faculty?
Pure necessity. I'd returned from France, where I'd spent three years under the G.I. Bill, I had a young son and wife to support, and I applied for a job, received it, and began to teach. I'd had prior teaching experience working with gifted children at New York University's Clinic for the Social Adjustment of the Gifted, but I'd never taught in college before. At that time I was fortunate in getting a position.

Were there other factors related to your entering the teaching profession at the time you came to it? (It's not Pennsylvania State we're talking about, is it?)
No, I was teaching at the State University of New York at Alfred.

How old were you at that point?
I was twenty-eight years old.

Were there other factors involved, then, besides security?
I'd come back from Paris and I was not trained for anything. I had never worked in my life at any job and I began teaching at a settlement house on the lower east side of New York. The salary

was $100 a month and I subsisted on that. We had a $14-a-month apartment; but the road would lead to nowhere. There was no place to work.

Teaching then (as now) offers a creative individual one avenue of subsistence and coexistence with creative work. The amount of time one puts into teaching still leaves the creative person with enough energy to be something more than a Sunday painter. Perhaps you might be a Tuesday, Thursday, Saturday, Sunday painter. But that is significant. That of course is the reason for going into university teaching and for continuing with it.

And of course there are some artists whom you know much better than I who believe that living in New York is the only way to go, so they take a job in a warehouse for forty hours a week, and claim that their commitment to art is very great because they are living in New York and somehow pursuing their work. I'd think that they don't really have very many hours or very much energy left.

New York is a stimulating city. I'm a native New Yorker, but I have no desire to live there now. I think the reasons are manifold. You know the phrase "to make it"; for painters, New York is the marketplace, the area of the highly influential museums, the collectors, galleries, critics. They feel that by being there, things will open if they just show great talent. Everybody has this tremendous belief in themselves. The tendency is to want to go to where they feel the action is.

But I don't feel that's necessary. I left New York. I began to work in the "provinces," and I achieved some degree of recognition without ever having to return to New York. It had always been my dream to go back to New York. But there are other reasons I think. I always thought of New York as a stimulating city: museums, galleries, restaurants, theaters, concerts, all these great offerings that one misses in the "provinces." But I don't feel the compelling interest and I don't think it's necessary. I think it's a great place to visit for stimulation, for recharging the batteries, but not necessarily to work there.

You've been teaching now since 1952. What do you like about it and what do you not like about it?

I'll be going back and forth, perhaps, between the two. The most interesting thing about teaching, I think, is the students. Let me say this with qualification: I've been teaching in state universities (this is the fifth one I've taught in) and while one does come across the gifted student and the exciting student every once in a while, the pickings are on the average mighty slim. I like the challenge of exciting, talented students. Mediocrity can be very discouraging. When the bulk of your students are mediocre, that's unfortunate. But occasionally you do run across that small percentage of individuals who make the whole thing worthwhile.

There are, of course, some students who are hopeless to begin with. But others from other disciplines have an avid interest in what is going on in the class and do very well. My feeling is when the student comes in, I do not grade toward a certain level; I grade the student on the rate of accomplishment since he or she entered the class. Each individual is solely that—an individual, and in the creative area you cannot do it as you do it in a math class.

I'm trying to figure out what is the difference as you see it between the good student, the exciting student, the one you're glad to see in the class, and those who are not welcome. What are some of the essential differences?

I like a student with a fierce sense of independence, with an approach that wants to say something about the world that student is living in, but doesn't look to the teacher for the stimulation, for the spoon-feeding. I'm thinking about the student who would interest me the most.

Naturally, in working with a student I don't attempt to give him a formula; each good student has something within himself which I try to help bring out. I don't attempt to have a class of followers. My own experience at art schools was pertinent. Sometimes I worked with teachers of reputation who had little to offer as teachers; they were competent artists but never really gave to the students. And sometimes I worked with people who were not known but had an approach that was understanding and very helpful to me as a student.

One of the most important experiences I had was a brief encounter with Josef Albers when I was at Black Mountain College in 1946. I was never an abstract artist, I was always figurative, and I felt that Albers would be very cold and indifferent to my work. But I found a great understanding; that precise Germanic mind of his reached in. I remember when he saw my work he looked at it for a long time in silence and then he said, "You are a poet," and then proceeded to criticize in a way that was extremely helpful. So it isn't necessary that a student be working in one's own direction.

I try to give to students. Sometimes it's discouraging, and sometimes it's encouraging. Sometimes it's poignant—particularly in these last few terms. There seems to be a dislocation of the student and some of the statements are really quite arresting. They don't know where they're going or why they're here; they're just drifting in a sense, and it's touching. I remember one particular boy last term who was like that, but I couldn't do anything for him. He came in a few times and just disappeared.

Then let me ask you very bluntly what I've been trying to find out: Are you more interested in students in your class as human beings (broadly speaking) or as artists in embryo?

I'm more interested in them as artists in embryo, because as human beings I think everybody is interesting, more or less. There just isn't the possibility of reaching them on full steam at that level. The time doesn't permit it. If you have a studio class you meet with twice a week, the lectures (I use the word loosely; let's call it informal talks) take up some of the time, then much of it is individual criticism. You cannot probe too deeply; sometimes you can, but it is very limited.

Is the whole setup a little too phony to be humane?

Not phony, but perhaps we're just scratching the surface. Unless one has a lengthy contact with an individual, I don't think you can really get to know each other, particularly when you're handling so many courses a year and scores of students go through your hands.

What is your role, then, as a teacher when a student comes to your class who isn't an artist in embryo but is willing and capable of learning from you? What are you supposed to do then?

It's very simple. As in singing—we all are capable of singing with varying degrees of competence. Some people, of course, have splendid voices and sing beautifully, but that doesn't mean that the rest of us should stop singing. I have this attitude in the visual arts. The person may be limited in his capacity to express himself visually, but he must sing as best he can, and if I can help in any way, I'll do so. That's the only way you can really solve the dilemma of the student who is not an artist in embryo.

I even tell that to the classes, too, because people are aware of their limitations.

We were talking about satisfactions and dissatisfactions and the first thing you mentioned was students. What else?

Another satisfactory phase of university life is the fact that one does have time to work creatively. The unsatisfactory things—I'm afraid this happens very often—the red tape, the administration, the departmental politics, the things that occur in a bureaucratic system, become quite disturbing and time-consuming.

Many people, not just artists, bitch and grumble about bureaucracy and departmental politics. I should think it would be possible for a person like you, who has made his mark on the world, who has a certain renown, to join a department and remain entirely aloof from the bureaucratic game-playing and politics if you wanted to.

Yes, I was aloof for a few years until about a year and a half ago, when the faculty organized to set up a system of self-government which was very good. I'm participating even to the point that I'm part of a triumvirate of three senior professors who will run the department while we search for a new man. This is reprehensible in me: I never wanted to do any administration. Meetings were things I've always avoided, and I've avoided going on any committee because I like to leave often. I work abroad, in Paris.

In fact, I don't have to teach. I can live off my work; could have lived off my work for many years. One of the things I want to do is reduce my teaching to a point where it becomes more tolerable in terms of time: perhaps two quarters a year, or one quarter a year; perhaps no quarters a year if I feel I won't miss certain aspects of university life.

Why have you stayed here these years? You've told me you don't have to work for the money.

Several reasons. While one doesn't have to have the money, one always has a sense of insecurity. If one sells one's work, markets can disappear. The American public can be very fickle; yesterday's hot artist is today's dead artist, figuratively speaking. I've seen it occur with many, many friends. Of course the work of these people that I've seen it happen to was of the moment, a trend: abstract expressionism, op, or pop, and they were perhaps third- or second-string people, but they were still competent people. But when the notoriety left, when that area was abandoned and became history, they were abandoned too, by the galleries and by the public that bought them.

Also, I have had pretty good leaves of absence and sabbaticals to go to France which have made the situation tolerable.

I don't mean that when I get a grant I suddenly become a productive individual. I had a nineteen-month leave of absence with a sabbatical and a few other things thrown in, and for the first ten months I didn't work—productively, that is. It bothered me for a while; then I thought, "What the hell? I'm living and enjoying myself." I worked in the garden and did things that are important that I never had taken the time to do before.

I don't know where I'd go. I used to think I'd like to live in

Paris. While I enjoy the city and speak French fluently, I still feel like a transient there; I don't know whether I'd like to live there. If I knew of an area in which I could live peaceably and yet be within range of stimulating activity, where I could move the mountains of this area, say, to within an hour's distance of New York, that would be ideal: to be able to partake of the city and drive back one hour and be in another world. We thought that sometime if I stopped teaching we'd go up to Connecticut, get something there and be in commuting distance of New York. But this is a very complex thing; many decisions would have to be made, many indecisions would have to be overcome.

One thing that is stimulating about the university is that the artist has the opportunity to meet people in other disciplines, and an interchange of ideas, warm friendships ensue. This has been very good in the nineteen years I have been teaching; I've enjoyed that enormously. Another thing I have enjoyed is the activism on the campuses. It's a very healthy sign.

There's nothing really bugging you other than the things you've mentioned so far?

Maybe I'm in a peaceable mood; I just had a great salary raise. One thing that bugged me in the past was the lack of appreciation for the creative arts in the university. In this university in particular, the sciences were *the* important thing. Of course the recent depression, recession, or lack of support the sciences received from foundations might have cast them in a new light on this campus. People suddenly began looking around and seeing that there are other areas too that have been attempting to maintain their own in spite of inadequate funding.

You know art is a frill; music is a frill. But making that better computer and finding a better insecticide is important. I'd like to see a change occur toward greater support for the arts, financial and philosophical.

You began by saying there was a certain lack of appreciation for the arts and artists on university campuses and I'm curious how that has been manifested in your own case? How do you know that's true?

In my case, it would be a recitation of neglect for years. I have a national reputation in my field. I was never given any consideration financially. Contact-hour-wise, my load was always maintained. For example, I feel to a certain extent that when in other departments renowned scientists teach a limited amount of time and do research the rest of the time, this is standard procedure. The man has proven himself as an investigator, as a creative scientist, and he is rewarded by the university's putting him on research. They are supporting his efforts. This has never occurred to any great degree here. The maximum I've had from the university is research support for two quarters; I never had anything as substantial as a full year given for research.

What I would like to have had is quiet time each term with university-sponsored research. This is very important. Now I'm speaking for myself personally, but there are others in the department who I can see that occurring with. I mean the university is completely insensitive.

When I was at Wisconsin, for example, I had two Guggenheims. At Wisconsin, the Central Research Fund was willing to augment it with half-salary for a year. Guggenheim grants are not bonanzas by any means. They were very small (now they are up to $10,000, but this was ten years ago when they were half that). Wisconsin was aware that an individual with a family could not survive on that.

At this university I received a similar grant. It was a Fulbright scholarship. Not a cent from here. There was no understanding whatsoever, no assistance given. I felt maligned. I felt that the university was taking advantage of the prestige I brought to them. It wasn't a reciprocal street.

I wasn't a showpiece, I don't want to be an "artist-in-residence." I was working and continuing to work, but I wanted some time. Everything that I did I had to fight for myself, get it by my own means. I happened to sell my work. But what if I didn't sell my work? I'd still be creating, I'd still need that support. Well, I could afford to give myself, say, a year off or take a couple of terms off. But the university never helped.

Has there been any conflict between you and your colleagues as a result of your strong reputation?

That exists, sure. I once heard a colleague of mine at Wisconsin make a remark about someone that I thought was very appropriate. He said, "The only thing I envy about him is his success." That probably exists.

Perhaps I'm appearing pretty sweet; I have very forceful views about creative work in general. I'd say that in most art departments throughout the country, perhaps less than a fraction of 1 percent are worth a damn (I'm speaking of teaching faculty), who have something to say, are good artists. The rest just don't have it. And that applies to my faculty, it applies to all the faculties I've taught on and all that I've seen. There are very few university artists of superior quality. There are lots of people who are dead as artists.

Some of them are good, warm human beings; they just never had it. They try, but they just don't. I'm sure that the criticism "He's commerical" is leveled at me, you know.

Don't they say that about anybody who sells?

Right, exactly. They always say that about anybody they *know* who sells anything. I don't have a persecution complex, but I know this: when you come to a campus as a visitor, if you have a reputation, you are tolerated because you're in, you're out, and you're away. But when you come as a permanent member and if you achieve success and recognition, and if your shows, your awards, your collections mount, and if this information is distributed (which in some cases it is), lots of people don't like it.

We have a research-contribution booklet the university publishes, and I had a very good year. At the time I was shooting for a full professorship here and I put it all down. It appeared in the book, and my colleagues had a line or two—shows at little local colleges and things like that. I had this long list. I remember a friend said, "Gee, your colleagues must hate you." In a sense, that sums it up. If you are there permanently and you achieve success, there might be some feelings of jealousy.

Would you go to a liberal arts college in the middle of Kansas then, where you would be a one-man art department?

No I wouldn't. I wouldn't go to the middle of Kansas for anything. Pick another area. That doesn't sound appealing at all. You see, one of the things you look for, in spite of certain differences with colleagues, when tradesmen get together there is something about that which is pleasant.

My wife is a creative artist and a good one. We miss the stimulation of artists we respect. It's a funny thing: among artists who have recognition (or we could use the phrase "have made it") there seems to be a rapport. I respect many of my colleagues. Occasionally we have a visitor who will come, and if we're fortunate in getting someone of quality, it's a wonderful ten weeks while he's here: we enjoy each other, see each other, and have much to give. I wish that people like that were here constantly; this is something we miss. We would have it, perhaps, if we were living in a place like Paris or New York—a steady diet of friends in the trade whom you respect. You have something to give each other. It's very important.

Let's play utopia for a minute. Tell me what your view of the ideal relationship between the artist-teacher and his institution might include.

I studied at Black Mountain College in North Carolina. Black Mountain was, perhaps, a place where the arrangement was very close to ideal inasmuch as every student had a studio. Their studios would be visited by faculty. Classes or talks were held informally. No such thing as attendance and grades or stuff like that. When a student was ready to be graduated from Black Mountain, experts in the discipline of the student were called in and spoke with the student for two or three days and if they felt he was to be graduated, he was graduated. It was an interesting school, and I think something like that, speaking of utopia, could exist—a kind of informality without the rigmarole and regulatory acts.

I don't believe in grades anyway—total nonsense. I have people who are hard-working students; I have people who are fuck-ups. I don't even like to be put in the position where I have to take someone who's just along for the ride. I try to turn him off; if he's wasting his time, I'm not going to waste my time when he shows up at the end of six weeks and shows me a few things. I tell him to take it out. I'm not interested. It's not a correspondence course; I want some contact with the student. He can best use me if I can see the thing as it develops: I see his thought processes, and I understand how he's going about it rather than seeing the finished work. With work presented when finished, the scaffolding is gone; one doesn't see the thought processes. I can help somebody if I see an inaccuracy in concept. I had a grad student last term who was an interesting fellow. He spent the entire term doing a massive drawing on the canvas on which he was going to paint. And then he proceeded to paint little tiny bits of it at a time. Gently, I kept on reiterating that it's impossible to complete a section of a canvas and have it relate to the entire thing. He was painting the details. I use a very simple metaphor when I have a class, and it applies to anybody. I try to have students think of something they're working on in the very same way they would if they were looking at a boat approaching a dock. From a distance, they see the large shape of the boat. As the boat gets closer, they begin to distinguish the deck. Closer still, the portholes. Closer still, the rivets on the portholes, and closer still, the scratches on the rivets. This is how one organizes one's work—if you have the concept of the big thing in the beginning and then go to secondary areas, and then to a still more minor area there, and then finally to the ultimate details. This way, you're in complete control of the whole thing as you work.

It appears that you must like to teach.
   Sometimes. Sometimes I don't.

When not?
   Well, I'm a human being, and some days I just don't feel like facing a group. I'd like to have the honesty to say, "Look, I

don't feel like talking today. You want to work, go ahead and work. I'll see you later."

Why don't you do that?

Occasionally I do. I have learned, though, to be dishonest in a sense within the system. I'm speaking of dishonesty in putting in an appearance and disappearing at a meeting—something like that.

As we're talking, I reflect—I think. I'm not telling you, really, about how very often I was completely discouraged. I don't dwell on things that are disturbing. Like any human being, you sweep those under the carpet. But so many times I say to myself, "What the fuck am I doing in this university? What am I doing with these people here? Am I crazy or something?" This feeling has occurred to me at meetings.

I cannot stand meetings. To a certain extent I can't stand democracy, I'm afraid, where everybody starts putting in two cents' worth and time just goes by, and meetings last for hours and nothing is accomplished. I was bored at meetings from the very beginning.

To a certain extent, I owe to meetings the start of my career. Like many young artists, I was influenced by outside success— what was current then. (It happened to be Picasso, twenty years ago when I began to teach.) At meetings I would doodle, draw. These drawings were something that were *not* Picasso; they were *my* personal things. I happened to send some in to an exhibition the Museum of Modern Art was holding called "Recent Drawing: U.S.A." There were thousands of works sent in, and they took about a hundred, and mine was one. I was overjoyed, you know: the Museum of Modern Art in New York.

I went in to see the show that summer, and there was a little red star on the drawing. "God, someone bought it!" I asked who had bought it. They said, "Why the museum did." This so encouraged me that I went in a few months later with the drawings and asked the curator if he'd like to see them. Not only did he see them, he sold them all. People on the staff there bought them, and secretaries bought them, trustees bought them, and

Nelson Rockefeller bought them. It all came from a boring faculty meeting: I should be grateful.

But I'm not grateful anymore. They're really terrible. I just can't stand them.

We're not having too much luck with our utopia. Let's try it another way. Say I'm trying to hire you away from here; what properties would a school need to attract you?

A small student body. I think one of the inadequacies of a large class is that you don't really get to know an individual as a human being. If one had ten or so people to work with (even that's a large number), one could draw out. There would be a two-way street. The individual would take something from you and you would get something from the individual. It's like knowing people: you know, at large parties there is so much going on that you don't really get to know the people. But if you have a small group, there's a great interplay of ideas. The conversation has a chance to probe and go to something more than superficialities or introductories.

I am particularly interested in that in terms of the creative area, where discourse must exist between people. When you look at a work of art, if it were just a surface, just what's there, that would be relatively easy. But there are more things involved.

Someone asked Ben Shahn if they could watch him work because they wanted to observe how his mind worked as he was painting. He said, "You'll never understand. At the same time you see me do something on canvas, at the same moment there are hundreds of decisions that simultaneously are being made while this is being done."

I'd like the idea, though, of a small school, small classes. And adequate work space.

Also, the ability to travel with students. I could see going with a small group of students to a city, to museums, to galleries, to the studios of other artists, too. Something like this would be very good.

One important condition would be that in addition to the art department there, I'd like to see other creative areas. I'd like to see a good theater arts program, a good music program, all of these things would abound. I'd like to see journalism, the political science area, history.

We began with the premise that this would be an attractive school. Now then, you either have to trust an administrator to get things done and hope that it will just happen to correspond with your ideal situation, or else you have to help. Now you've been saying that you don't like meetings, you don't like bureaucracy, you don't like administration. As far as I know, nobody has discovered a way to shape a school's destiny (after all, we're talking about a social institution) without some meetings. We're going to have to discuss curriculum, we're going to have to engage some other people to teach, and things like that to get our ideal situation. So what about it; are you willing to do that?

Well, I have here, and if it's important enough, yes. But like the petty things, such as how many credit hours this is worth, so on and so forth, and grades, etc. . . .

I think it takes a meeting of the minds, an agreement, to abolish grades and credit hour requirements.

I'd be willing to meet on important things. I have and I do.

You'll go to meetings where an artistic decision can be made and then implemented?

And also political decisions. For example, if we're voting for senators or something where I feel an individual is the right kind of man for the senate, I'll go in and vote or support him.

We've had these meetings concerning how to have an adequate department. I've worked with the faculty on that. I realize that things don't just run themselves and my role is not simply to gripe and applaud; I have to do something to make things run smoothly, and I'm in there for that.

How do you think your own work has been affected by your affiliation with a university art department?

It's completely separate from it; never in any way influenced by anything in the university; no connection whatsoever.

That's all you want to say?

It's true. Once during a very disagreeable period (the most traumatic period of my life) it was affected. It was very hard to work—almost impossible. They were attempting to remove me, and brought a series of charges up. There was extreme jealousy. It was a question of revolt there.

One of the charges was that I was more interested in the gifted student than in the mediocre. I said, "Guilty. Absolutely guilty." Another charge was that certain students were afraid to take Mr. Altman's courses because they felt he was too demanding. I said, "Fine." Some of these charges were really ridiculous. There was an old maid at registration (that was one of the awful duties one had there; you were a clerk). I did some small drawings of an erotic nature. I was very careful not to offend the old biddies; they saw them and said that these were dirty drawings. I brought them into the dean and he said, "I'd like to own them." They weren't dirty; he thought they were delightful. It was incredible.

This affected me very much. My work is of a very serene nature and maybe the very fact that I turn to something like that—the world may be falling down, and here I draw just a single individual sitting in a park. How strange.

On the whole this kind of trauma doesn't come very regularly?

No, it doesn't. But I've seen people that were profoundly affected by it.

But you aren't one of them?

Not really. It doesn't eat at me inside slowly. It just explodes. Watch out. But I've learned how to fight in situations.

Regarding your own work, you don't feel that the university placed such demands on your time that your own work was affected adversely?

Yes. This is contradictory now. In the beginning, I was not demanding of the university and made certain sacrifices. One of the sacrifices I made was the "living" bit. I remember speaking to a friend, a poet. I was telling him how I felt about teaching, I had to teach, and I had this strong compulsion to work. And yet I also wanted just to live—just to walk through the woods and play with my son or do something. With these tremendous pressures I had to sacrifice one for the other. He told me, "These things are very necessary, very important to you. You must do them." So it does affect you.

I want more of these things. I want to enjoy life as well as to work and fulfill my teaching. That's why I speak of reducing the teaching I do have. I was contemplating once going to another school, the University of Maryland, and I liked the fact that they assume that their senior professors are productive and they give them *more* time to work rather than less.

The attitude here has been like a democracy. (I told you I don't like democracy. I don't believe in a democracy of talent. I don't believe in democracy in all senses of the word.) Everybody works the same amount of time; beginning instructors work the same amount of time as the full professor. But the full professor also has a hell of a lot of other things he has to do. It's not right. That's something I'd like to change here. I'd like to teach one course instead of two or three.

What is it that the art department here is trying to do vis-à-vis students? What are its goals? What do you hope your output might be at the end of four or six years?

I think that, at best, the university can only give a smattering of everything; a taste of this and a taste of that and no more than that. It cannot possibly cover everything. You have to make a choice: either you attempt to put out a well-rounded Renaissance Man, or you attempt to put out someone who has at least a quasi-professional standing when he graduates.

I think that a small taste in certain areas will have to do. Education is not just something that ends when you get your degree. It's a continuing, lifetime process. I think it is a good thing to drop some courses. We're leaving them as options for those people who feel the need.

I always felt it totally inadequate, this smattering of painting that the student got, this little bit of drawing. When I went to school, I went to Cooper Union from nine to five during the day, I went to the Art Students League at night from seven to ten, I went to another school on Saturday. On Sunday, to amuse myself, I painted. I mean that was my life, and I was really involved in it. There's no involvement to speak of here in universities. When you do find involvement, you find a good student. The thing that takes them away from this involvement is papers they have to write for other areas and whatnot and there's a conflict there.

Basically, what we're talking about then is general, liberal education versus professional education. Where do you stand there?

What I consider a decent balance; I'd like to see as much professional education as one can possibly give to the student and fulfill the maximum requirements of general education.

Have you felt any kind of limitations in your experience as a result of lack of a broad, liberal education?

No, not at all. I don't feel any limitation. But in terms of the students here, I advise them to get degrees because, while I'm teaching in a university system and have risen, I know how difficult it is when these people are candidates for jobs. I came with talent and not much recognition and got a job.

One of the things I think sad, though, is people going out with a new degree and the first thing they do is teach. I'd like to see them get some experience—do a little living. I think five years of living would be a requisite; then start teaching. I began teaching when I was twenty-eight, but we have candidates with their new master's degrees getting jobs. They've just been taught and they start teaching, and there's nothing that they're teaching from, no real "on-their-ownness" that I'd like to see.

If we are in agreement that the artist-teacher does a special thing for the place where he is, I'm wondering if you can help me understand how the university might elicit more commitment from first-class producing artists to teaching? (I'm talking about individuals exactly like yourself.)

Utilize them in such a way that you don't tax their energies. Give them a chance for stimulating teaching. That is, give them a good student body; the university should be critically aware of the type of student it is admitting to professional-level courses. (You wouldn't expect Nadia Boulanger to take someone who is going to play "Chopsticks.") You want a "master class" in a certain sense: more capable students.

Also an awareness of the creative individual as a faculty member who is going to make a specific contribution to the university department; he will not serve on committees. He's going to make his contribution. His work, and the discipline, understanding, and creativity that go on in his studio come with him as he walks into the classroom.

Give him adequate time and optimum conditions for research; these two simple things I think are absolutely requisite.

Leslie Bassett

Leslie Basset was born January 22, 1923, in Hanford, California. He studied at Fresno State College (B.A.), the University of Michigan (M.Mus., A.Mus.D.), and the Ecole Normale in Paris.

Important recognition has come through the Pulitzer Prize, Prix de Rome, Fulbright, and Koussevitzky Foundation awards. He received a citation and grant from the National Institute of Arts and Letters, UNESCO, and other awards.

Mr. Bassett's works have been performed by European orchestras and the orchestras of Boston, Chicago, Cleveland, New York, Philadelphia, and other ensembles and soloists.

Mr. Bassett is chairman of the composition department at the University of Michigan.

How was it, Mr. Bassett, that you decided to become a teacher?

I think I grew up as a teacher, really. I've liked music ever since I can remember. I studied piano as a kid; in high school I studied trombone and enjoyed playing in orchestras and bands. I admired my high school music teacher, and when I entered college I elected a music education curriculum because there was no other way to earn a living in music at that time.

Were you thinking of yourself as a composer during your undergraduate years?

No. This gradually emerged. I always dabbled in composing but never had any real instruction. But during three and a half years in the army I did a lot of arranging. Arranging, if you carry it far enough, comes very close to composing. In fact, you enjoy the introductions and the endings and the bridges that you've made yourself in the works that you've arranged and you hate to use the borrowed material. Eventually, what you do is throw out the initial stuff and you have a composition. So after getting out of the army, I was much interested in composition. As a veteran I could really study it. So I began graduate work and one thing led to another. I became a teaching fellow, and I had a Fulbright to France, from which we returned stone broke and in debt, so in order to live I got a teaching job in California in the public schools. I then was offered a position here which was to be temporary; I was to be here only two years. But here I still am, you see. There were opportunities to leave, but I always felt it was professionally more exciting to remain here. We had the Stanley Quartet, which played my music, and faculty colleagues played it. Because of that professional excitement and because I'd been trained as a teacher (after all, it seemed perfectly normal to be a teacher), this seemed a compatible combination of two professions.

Composing and teaching just evolved together then?

Right. Because of military service, my undergraduate career was spread out over seven years. Loathsome as it was, military service—playing trombone and arranging—helped me get a picture of what professional music life might be like. Had I just gone straight through school, acquired my teaching certificate, I probably then would have got a teaching job where I might perhaps still be at this point.

Do you wish you could earn enough money through composing so that you could live decently without having to teach?

At times, yes. But on the whole I think that would be perilous. There are times when one wants to get away privately and do his own work: be able to resolve the things he needs to resolve as a composer. You can't do that if daily challenges are forever coming to you.

The other side of it, of course, is that if I were never exposed to young people and new ideas, never challenged as somebody who is not progressing—the way young people challenge you—I think it would be the professional death of me. It would be a bad thing, and you see this in a lot of composers who don't have this kind of affiliation.

What composer now living in the United States could survive decently solely on income from his work? Mr. Copland?

Yes, I should think so. There was a survey made ten or twelve years ago by B.M.I. or A.S.C.A.P. on the income of as many composers as they could think of. As I remember it, there were five or six who were earning enough money to live on. There were quite a few who were earning enough to nicely supplement their other income. Times have changed since then, of course. I suppose anybody who's doing music for television is doing quite well.

But if we limit it to what we think of as "art" music or serious music—what we think of as the composer's art—are there others besides Copland who could earn enough money to have a good life?
I haven't thought about it too much. I think there must be several, but almost everyone I can think of has a professorship, or some kind of guest composer status, or he's a conductor, or he publishes "conversations with somebody" or somehow supplements his income. I think maybe it isn't all because they need the money; maybe they just enjoy it. I certainly enjoy going someplace as a guest composer; I do this five or six times a year.

That's what motivated the question, of course. All the important living composers in this country seem to have a connection with a university or, to a lesser extent, a conservatory.
It's the patron of our day. It's the professional patron: it's where the performers are. Most all performances of my music are given in some university.

If somehow you got a sum of money so substantial that you would never have to concern yourself about finances again, would you continue to teach?
I don't know. I suppose I might look at the alternatives. But I'm afraid I might feel professionally orphaned. My life has been so tied to the university (in fact my whole mature professional career has been tied to *this* university) that after having taught for quite a few years, you begin to notice a certain redundancy. You find yourself saying certain things over and over because they need to be said.

If you only had brilliant students, this would of course be a delight. You'd just use them as colleagues. My good students are all "colleagues"; my poor students are "students." Now I could do without "students," but "colleagues" I need.

It's a very curious thing, though, how the "flavor" of students changes markedly from year to year. The interest composer groups have in what is studied, what music we look at, the kinds of things that interest them—these are the exciting things about teaching, of course. Anybody who's not connected with young composers misses out on something there: there's a vitality of music *now* he's not getting.

All composers I know teach. Perhaps it's because they primarily need a secure income, but not far down the list is because they need stimulus from young colleagues.

What is the most frustrating element in your university affiliation?

I suppose I would have left university life if I'd found a constant element which had frustrated me from year to year. Every year something comes up, but if there is one threat, it's that the university can sometimes encroach on your composing time, on your life as a composer. That can wipe you out. I just refuse generally to appear at the university in the morning. I work at home mornings. We all urge our students to set up similar schedules, realizing that you need really sizable blocks of time to get anything done. I think a person has to save his freshest time in the day for his own work. If he doesn't do this, in five years' time he hasn't produced any work and is therefore of less value to the university as a composer. After ten years, he'd be of no value to anybody—including himself. He'd have ceased to be a composer.

It's the same with performers. They can be so loaded that they can't practice, and can't go on tours, and it's a pernicious thing. What you end up with is only teachers. Now teachers are fine, but the thing you're teaching is a message to the public. Now how can a teacher teach how to reach the public if he doesn't do it anymore?

I don't have any major complaints. I would just sometimes like a little more time for my composing and a little less time for the university. Perhaps that's selfish, but I don't really think it is.

Sometimes a man of considerable prominence—professional prominence—in a department can evoke from colleagues a certain amount of hostility or jealousy. Have you ever noticed any of that?

It never bothered me in the least. I'm not aware of this as a problem. My colleagues are distinguished people in their own right. I don't think there's jealousy in any respect. I suppose this could exist someplace, but I think it's a sick thing. All a composer has to do to cure himself of any feelings of inferiority is start a new piece. When he starts a work, he believes that's the finest piece in the world. He's excited by it. He's not worried about what somebody else is writing. It's only in those periods between pieces when a person is looking around and feeling a bit impotent, having used up his ideas on his last piece and not formed his ideas for the next one, that he might look around and wish for some other's success. But I don't think that happens here, in any case.

Let me ask you what is probably the most important question: what do you think has happened to your own creative output as a result of your affiliation with a university?

I think on the whole university life has been stimulating to me as a composer. There have been certain fluctuations, naturally. The size of a catalog of works isn't important; it's the quality of the catalog that makes a difference. There's no guarantee that you're going to write a masterpiece no matter how many you crank out. A person could write six, or eight, or fifteen pieces a year and all of them could be junk ultimately. If you wrote one piece every six years and it were a masterpiece, you'd consider yourself very fortunate indeed.

For me, I can't imagine another life in which I could have done what I've done. I give great credit to having been in a university as a stimulus to my work. That's true in many ways. For example, I got a Fulbright and went to Paris and studied with Arthur Honegger and Nadia Boulanger. All of this was very exciting. Well you have to be in a university to get a Fulbright. I had the Rome prize; the university helped me financially, and I couldn't have taken it otherwise. There have been grants. I've had lots of recognition and commissions which wouldn't have come to me if I hadn't been in the university. You can trace the university's influence over a lot of what happened to me.

It seems to me that if a composer is excited and interested by his circumstances, this is all you can ask. You hope that you come up with good music. On the whole, I think the university has supplied me with more of those kinds of circumstances than I would have had in any other guise. I know it's the best connection for me.

Jorge Bolet

Jorge Bolet was born November 15, 1914, in Havana, Cuba. He studied at the Curtis Institute, and made his American debut at Carnegie Hall in 1933. In 1937 he won the Naumburg Award.

Currently Mr. Bolet is among the busiest pianists on the American musical scene, playing with major orchestras and in numerous recitals in all musical capitals of the world. Although his repertory is varied, he specializes in the virtuoso works of the Romantic period. He records for RCA.

Mr. Bolet teaches at Indiana University.

Mr. Bolet, I want to talk with you about your relatively new career as a faculty member in a university. Why did you become a teacher? What where the factors involved in your decision to join this faculty?

This is really not any new desire of mine. I always enjoyed teaching very much and I have felt that teaching is a very essential part of a performer's career. I think that we as performers have perhaps been able to solve a great many problems and it is our duty to pass on to other generations whatever "secrets" we might have garnered through the experience of performance before an audience. If I have not affiliated before with any conservatory or music school of a university, it is because every time I have been approached, the stipulations and the restrictions on my concertizing made it prohibitive. When Dean Bain approached me about coming to Indiana, I certainly ascertained beforehand that I would more or less be free to go on and concertize as I have been doing for almost thirty years now, as long as I made up absences. We have a certain number of weeks in each semester in which each student is supposed to have one lesson. Well, as long as each one of my students gets the required number of lessons, it really makes little difference when they get those lessons. They might get three lessons in one week and then not have any lessons for three weeks.

But the incentive, the thing that drew you here—was it principally that you wanted to teach?

Well, that was one of the incentives. Naturally, we can never get away from the other advantages in connection with a university like this. You know we as performers go through long, long periods in building our careers (unless you happen to be a Van Cliburn, who sort of struck it rich in his very early days), through very lean years where every penny that we make has to be invested right back in the career. A certain financial security is a great incentive to come and be affiliated with a university; our insurance program, our retirement plan, all those things I think are very attractive incentives.

You haven't been here very long, but I would like to know what you have liked about being a teacher in the university and what has annoyed you.

The one thing I find most enjoyable is the pleasure one gets from having students that really show results and progress and to see a student who might not have had too many musical advantages come and all of a sudden grow and blossom. That is a great reward. Next to that, I would mention personal contact and friendship with a marvelous faculty such as we have here at Indiana. Living the life of a concert performer is a rather lonely one, as you well know, and the opportunities for any kind of prolonged social contacts, professional musical contacts with your colleagues, are really far between—especially in my case. I never really enjoyed living in a very large metropolis. I lived in New York for several years after the war but then I got completely fed up. Now I never go to New York unless I am performing in New York or around the New York area. I moved out to the San Francisco Bay area but there again I was not in San Francisco, I was forty miles away. From there I moved to a little fishing village up on the north coast of Spain, which to me is really the ideal place to live and it's where I intend to retire when I am no longer wanted anywhere. Living like that, the chances of any kind of intensive social, musical atmosphere are really not very frequent.

Let's try to separate those out for a few minutes—the social from the musical. I am interested in your colleagues here and your reaction to them. Here there are people with first-class international reputations. Do you think that you could ever have been attracted or would you go now to an institution which hadn't on its faculty such "stars"?

No, I don't believe so.

You need to have that kind of intellectual and musical interaction with people of your own rank and caliber.

Yes, exactly. I think that is really one of the great attractions that Indiana University has.

OK, then are you willing to say that you don't have any missionary zeal?

No. I can't say that I am that much of a missionary. I just can't conceive of myself in that kind of role.

What are some of the reasons?

Well, I believe very firmly that in order to grow and in order to maintain your standards at the very highest level, you need the challenge of—you might use the word "competition." In a place where you are the big fish in a little pond, the situation would be rather stagnating and it would remove a great deal of that drive that I think we must have in order to become always greater, always finer, always deeper. You know a musician, a performer, has to grow. I think the minute that you stop growing you start rotting, and I think that could happen in a small college or university with an undistinguished music department as opposed to what we have here.

A few people have said that the artist is an alien figure in the university and in academic life in general. How does it make you feel to be a faculty member here with credentials that are not ordinary ones?

Well, I think academic life as such can be rather stultifying and suffocating. A great deal of academic life revolves around such a small, local kind of world that you sort of start swimming with your head lower and lower until eventually you are swimming under water all the time. Academics live in a world of their own and they have so little notion and so little contact with any world outside of academe.

That really doesn't happen here in the music school because, as you very well know, there are any number of full professors at this school of music who don't even have a bachelor's degree. So in a strict sense we are not bound or circumscribed by academic criteria. We are more or less a world unto ourselves, and if we are here it's because we add distinction and prestige to the university as a whole and to the school of music in particular.

We began talking about your satisfactions and dissatisfactions in university life and the first thing you mentioned was teaching and the students and their development. Why do you like that?

Well, it's not a question of teaching perhaps as much as a question of being able to hear performances other than your own which come up to your same high standards and ideas about music. I enjoy hearing other people's students as much as I enjoy hearing some of my own for the simple reason that every time I go to a performance of music regardless of where it is or who it is, I am always anticipating the very highest that there is in music.

I guess it all depends on the personality and the makeup of the teacher. I can only speak for myself, but I must say that I have a rather natural tendency to become personally involved with my students and with their problems outside of music. But I think there is a great danger in becoming too involved. I believe as far as possible we must keep a certain detachment so that we can look at the student purely as a human being with x amount of talent and the potential to which that talent can be developed. There are many things that you have to do in teaching students. You must analyze their character and their makeup, their reaction to certain circumstances and so on, in order to teach them most effectively.

Do you think you are a good teacher?

Well, I believe I am. You know, there are many, many performers who are what I call "intuitive musicians." They seem to know music and they seem to feel music through an inborn instinct and they know things and they do things which no one has really taught them. I studied very briefly with Rosenthal. Now here was a great pianist, a great artist, a great musical personality. He was a student of Liszt, you know, a man who you would think would have so much to say about any piece of music that any student played for him. (I must say he was terribly expensive. A friend of mine fortunately paid for my lessons at the time because I certainly could never have afforded them.) But I cannot tell you one single thing that this man ever told me. He never told me anything. I would arrive at his villa and "What are you going to play for me today?" "Well, the *Appassionata*." "Oh, good. Fine. Wonderful." So I would sit down and play the *Appassionata* from beginning to end. "Um, that's very good, that's very nice. Now what else are you going to play for me?" These were his lessons. I played for him vast amounts of repertory: the Liszt Sonata; the Chopin ballades, scherzi, sonatas; Beethoven sonatas. Everything was "fine."

One thing I do recall his telling me: he pointed out very clearly what a bad composer Liszt was, and this rather amazed me because I should think he would have had Liszt on the highest pedestal. Well, that's the only thing I ever recall his telling me.

Now, you see, I am not that kind of musician. I am not an intuitive musician. I think I have a certain intuition for music but my intuition is more for the mechanical aspect of piano-playing, having had always a very great facility. But my facility for appreciating purely musical values and aesthetic values and emotional values, I must confess, I have had to receive from other people. I have always been a very analytical student of music and of piano-playing and in order to learn those musical values and in order to appreciate them and absorb them and be able to project them with conviction in my own playing, I have had to analyze and scrutinize things down to the cell within a cell within a cell, so that whenever I play, I assure you that I have a very exact road map of everything. So when it comes to teaching, you see, I don't believe in using the kind of teaching where one student sits at one piano and I sit at the other piano. When I am teaching I am generally sitting so that I can watch their hands. I go to the piano to illustrate only after I have explained to them what I mean and what I am trying to get across. I mean this idea of "do it this way" is no good. I think if you say, "Do it this way," the pupil has a perfect right to ask, "Why?"

You take teaching very seriously, don't you?

Oh! I certainly do! Perhaps I take it too seriously. I have been told that by some of my colleagues here.

You know, basically, there are no great teachers. There are only great students. I think that is the great secret and in that consists the great fame of some of the great pedagogues of the piano. I think prime examples in this country are Lhévinne, Genhart, and Marcus for example. They had the good luck because of their name and fame to attract the very greatest talents. I only hope that someday I will really have a good number of great talents at this school because I am very curious to see what a greatly talented student would play like after having studied with me for three or four years.

It's a fascinating prospect, isn't it?

Yes, it really is. It's not that I am looking for a vicarious pleasure of hearing something that I can't do myself. I think there have been too many teachers in the past who really got the only pleasure they had from their profession by hearing their students play because they couldn't do it themselves. That's rather sad. I think you then get into all kinds of unhealthy, personal, psychological problems in your relations with your students.

Are there other things about university life which you would like to mention?

The whole musical atmosphere is one thing that I enjoy very much. As you say, Bloomington might be out in the middle of nowhere but when you are here, you really feel that you are right in the center of things. There are so many things going on all at once, it's just impossible. We have over 600 concerts and recitals every year and eight or more new opera productions every year.

It's a little early to tell, I guess, because you have only been here a few years, but I would like to know what you think has happened to your own professional career as a result of affiliation with this university?

Well, so far I have not detected any change. You know I have never been one of those artists who was booked solid from the last week in September until the last week in May.

I think we are all aware that you can count those artists on one hand.

Yes, that's right. And so far I must say there have been relatively few engagements that I haven't been able to accept. So far it's really worked out extremely well. Now I can see that perhaps sometime in the future I might have such a tremendous number of engagements that I really won't be able to carry on my load here, in which case I can just ask for a leave of absence for a semester. We can always get a substitute teacher to come in if it is necessary for us to be away for a more extended period of time.

It can be worked out if you are not a performer who has to play seventy to eighty dates a year. Then, of course, it's absolutely impossible because then you need every day of the playing year.

I guess the fundamental question in all this is, "Are you happy as a faculty member?" and so far, everything I have gotten from you has been "Yes."

Well, if you got that impression, it certainly is the correct one.

George Crumb

George Crumb was born October 24, 1929, in Charleston, West Virginia. He studied at the Mason College of Music, the University of Illinois (M.Mus.), and the University of Michigan (A.Mus.D.), and at the Hochschule für Musik in Berlin.

He received grants from the Rockefeller, Guggenheim, and Coolidge foundations, the National Institute of Arts and Letters Award, and the Pulitzer Prize. Of Mr. Crumb's works, "Ancient Voices of Children," "Black Angels," and "Night of the Four Moons" are among the most frequently performed pieces of contemporary music.

Mr. Crumb teaches at the University of Pennsylvania.

Mr. Crumb, how were you drawn into the teaching profession? How and why did you become a teacher?

I suppose my own experience is like that of many other composers: I found that a teaching career was compatible with doing my own creative work. It boils down to having time to work.

What do you like about teaching in a university?

I think the best thing that can happen is that you have some good students with interesting ideas about music and about composition. This I think can influence your own work in a very positive way. I think this is the one most exciting aspect.

What do you not like about university life and teaching?

I'm not sure there's anything specific. I do feel at times we're tied to a rather regular schedule, even though it may represent only a few hours per week of actual teaching time. Sometimes in composition, if things come to a head, you'd like to work all day long seeing through a project and it's a little hard to take off two months in the middle of a semester and interrupt one's teaching for this purpose.

Do you teach classes other than composition?

Yes, I have two classes in analysis of music. This has been my usual schedule here at Penn for several years.

Are you satisfied with that? Would you be happier teaching only composition, or only analysis, or is this the way you like it?

I've always felt that variety was a nice thing to have. As a matter of fact, next year I'll be teaching some undergraduate basic ear training and musicianship, which I haven't done in the past.

I'm really looking forward to that. I've often felt that much of our teaching in music is directed toward a visual, kind of intellectual approach, having to do with writing technique and analyzing music in an intellectual way. So it might be fun to go back to the listening and training of the ear in a very solid way.

Are there things other than the hamstringing of your time which you'd like to mention as annoying to you in university life and teaching?

I guess I feel there can exist a little bit of tension between your work in the university and your own creative work. But I happen to feel that tension can be a good thing. I think one will always write music in any situtation if one has to write music. The minimal amount of tension you might have in a university situation I think is not necessarily bad. I think it's probably rather good.

How has your own work been affected by your affiliation with the university, in terms of both quantity and quality?

I think I wouldn't be able to answer that. I'm not sure there's a direct relationship. I feel you write the music you have to write and this is in a dimension apart from whatever responsibilities you have. Students can be stimulating; you can get ideas, you know, raw materials, and you can test out ideas occasionally. But I think of the two areas as really quite independent.

Maybe I should define "tension," too. I didn't mean to imply animosity, say, on the part of administrators in the university. In our own case we have a composer as our chairman now who understands composers' problems, and I think he's very willing to work out schedules and so forth so that we can have the hours when we work best free for our own work. By "tension" I mean that in teaching you have to put yourself in a different frame of mind that I think is a different way of thinking about music than the creative way. Maybe not necessarily, but I feel in my case that it is. You have to be objective in a certain sense and try to verbalize things that you don't do in the creative process. You tend to think in terms of the elements that you're working with in a nonverbal way. You're in intimate touch with the materials of your art. There's not this impediment of having to verbalize what you're doing. It's an immediate process.

Tell me a little more about students. What kind of students do you not like (if there are any)?

I don't like indifferent students. I think whatever they're doing they should want to do well.

Do you mean "indifferent" students or "untalented" students?

Both, actually.

One might envision a student who is not particularly talented but who works. How do you respond to a student like that?

Well, I admire anybody who works. Sometimes you can compensate for lack of talent in a certain area (I mean given a minimal talent which you have to have, I suppose, in music). But there are many students who can make that go a long way. This is always exciting when it happens. We've had many excellent students at Penn. I think most of our students are very hard workers.

I'm trying to figure out whether you really like to teach. We've been going at it rather circuitously, I guess. Do you like to teach?

Yes and no. Sometimes I do; it can be exciting. Other times I don't. I think it has something to do with my willingness or unwillingness to verbalize about music. We all function on larger rhythms. Any part of our life is constructed this way, I think. Sometimes these rhythms don't always agree with what we're required to do.

Creativity, working in composition, is not just a matter of putting in four or five hours a day. You may go along for some months and not achieve very much; you may have a good week and write your year's worth of music, in a sense—at least conceptually you might develop within a week what it would take a year or two to carry out.

I'm interested in your feelings about having to verbalize about music. Do you not like to do it just because it's hard or do you have some deep-seated aesthetic objection to trying to verbalize about music?

I do have an objection: I think music is a language in its own right. I think healthy periods in music avoided this verbalization; it was enough for them to write the music and play it. Criticism, you know, in the nineteenth century didn't become an analytical intellectual approach to music; it was a rather poetic reaction to music.

I think it's the only sensible way to react to music, really. I can't imagine that people would really be interested in the technical minutiae involved in it.

That's interesting, but I'm surprised. I should think that as a composer, you'd prefer that a critic not say, "I don't like it." I should think you'd prefer him to say, "I don't like it because of such and such," in such a way that you might get a better understanding of his acceptance or rejection of the piece.

I can also see that you might think, "Well, his understanding of the working-out of the piece, the technique, the craftsmanship involved, is so poor that there's nothing he can say about it that would enlighten me in any way regarding his own personal reactions to it." Would you comment a little more about those two things?

I think that music is either well written, well founded, the craft is good, or it's not. Either it works or it doesn't. Also, I suspect that it's a little hard for me in my own mind to separate the so-called craft of composition and the conception or the fantasy and imagination. If you could imagine a composer improvising directly at the piano where things fall into place, he projects his ideas immediately without forethought. Maybe that illustrates what I'm getting at.

I think we make an artificial division in music: we tend to break it down into little compartments in our teaching. It should be all of one piece. I think, too, there are attempts in universities to intellectualize music to make it "respectable." That's the main danger to creative music in the universities. But if a composer has something to say, this shouldn't bother him at all; he goes his own way. It's just necessary to recognize the danger, to be aware that the danger exists.

You keep saying "intellectual" as if it were a dirty word.

No, it's not really. It's perfectly respectable when it's applied to scholarship or things that universities traditionally were competent, founded to do. Now, of course, the university has become universal. It includes arts—painting and music and so forth—and I don't think art is an intellectual discipline. Yet in order to accommodate itself within a university, it tends to want to justify its existence and become respectable. The musician wants not to feel inferior next to the historian.

Do you feel uncomfortable next to the historian in the university? Do you wonder whether you "fit"?

No, I really don't because I think I'm aware of that potential danger and I'm not aware that I'm trying to put myself into that category. I feel as comfortable as I would in any other situation.

Do you get along well with your colleagues here?

I get very much out of talking about music with my colleagues on the composition faculty. We get together frequently in a social way and just talk about music and play.

Do you think it's necessary to have a certain number of artists on a faculty for a composer such as yourself to be happy? Let me ask it another way: would you go to a school as a faculty member where you were a one-man music department?

No. I wouldn't enjoy a situation like that. I really would much prefer having colleagues whom I respect; you can bounce ideas around. We have that here. It seems comfortable and stimulating and of course there are a lot of large cities close by and it's possible to hear music and see other musicians, composers, perhaps more frequently.

Would you mind trying to idealize a relationship between an artist-teacher and his host institution? Don't feel bound by any kind of convention, tradition, or practicality. What would seem to you a utopian situation in that regard?

The artist has to have a schedule that's light enough so that he has time and energy to do his own work. The university should recognize that some of its people are creative and when they include these people on their faculties, they should make allowances. They do it for people who are doing research—this consumes untold extra hours of private time. The same situation exists with artists.

You said that the schedule ought to be such that the artist can do that for which he was engaged in the first place. What would be an ideal number of working hours? You now teach ten; what would you prefer as ideal?

I think no more than ten or twelve.

So in a sense your situation here at Pennsylvania is ideal for you in that regard.

Yes, I have no objections at all on this count.

What other qualities of this unique, ideal institution would make it so?

I think the administration should have a rather unstructured program in teaching music so that there's much flexibility for the individual teacher. I think this is a way to counteract an artificial division of music into departments where it becomes a rigid situation.

This might lead back to the old apprentice idea, where the student consults a number of hours a week with his teacher on a private basis and has no regular classes set up as such. This could be a rather interesting situation. I'm not sure it would work, but it might; it did in the past.

The conservatory has developed into a kind of ingrown thing in this country, in many cases. This is indicated by the fact that so many conservatories have now been assimilated into universities. There are very few left of any prominence. And there is another kind of danger that music loses touch with real life—that is, the rest of the world. Ideally, the university should influence artists in a universal sense. I think it would be a good thing if our composition students had a class in astronomy or archaeology; you can learn as much about composition that way as through some of the things we teach them.

I must say that I don't really think composition can be taught in any real sense. In a way we're pretending to do something that's impossible. I don't think composition ever was taught.

Can sociology be taught?

I'm not sure; I suppose it can. I think artistic fields, creative fields, cannot really be taught in the same sense as the other disciplines.

I'll not belabor this point, but I believe what you're maintaining is that craft and craftsmanship can be taught—but not creativity. That brings me back to the sociologist: I think Talcott Parsons might say that creativity in sociology is just as precious and elusive a thing as creativity in composing music, and that you can teach the craftsmanship involved and the technique necessary to becoming a good sociologist, but you can't teach creativity, which is necessary to becoming a great sociologist who makes a genuinely unique contribution to the field. Perhaps that's the common ground between the two.

I think you're right. You can teach some of the mechanics of composition.

*I'm curious about what role you think the music department at the
University of Pennsylvania is trying to play.*

We try to open possibilities. Let me speak about composition
first. We try to perform our students' music as much as possible. We react to their music. We try to acquaint them with
some music they perhaps are not familiar with; in some cases,
they acquaint us with music we're not familiar with. There's an
interchange among the people who are interested in music as a
creative thing. Attitudes rub off even if they're not directly
taught, in a subtle way. Hopefully it means something.

I think the objective of the department is to turn out people
who are more or less committed to music whether they are
musicologists or composers. The musicology training here is
fairly thorough. We turn out some committed students. The
standards, I think, are pretty high.

We have a Ph.D. in composition rather than a D.M.A. I'm really not convinced that any advanced degree makes much
sense. Again, it's kind of a thing that's developed. You know,
the students feel that they can't get a good teaching job without
a doctor's degree. I think we even make the situation worse by
calling it a Ph.D. and demanding a written dissertation rather
than a musical composition for a doctoral student.

*If you suddenly came into a large sum of money sufficient for all
your needs, would you still teach?*

I'm not sure; I've asked myself that question. I suppose it
would be useful to see how you would work in that situation. I
imagine you would feel the necessity of the kind of stimulation
that you get with students and faculty. Maybe you could find
that in other ways too—simply by keeping in touch with other
people who are writing music.

*I'm interested in whether artists are happy or unhappy in their
teaching situations. Which are you?*

I guess I'm generally happy. I really have no outstanding
complaints. I guess by nature unless things were terribly wrong

in some respect I probably wouldn't react strongly myself anyway. But I feel generally that at Penn we have a nice department: nice for the composers and nice for the students.

Kenneth Evett

Kenneth Evett was born December 1, 1913, in Loveland, Colorado. He studied at Colorado State College (B.A.), Colorado College (M.A.), and the Colorado Springs Fine Arts Center.

His paintings have been shown at national centers such as the Whitney Museum, the Metropolitan Museum of Art, the Art Institute of Chicago, the Pennsylvania Academy, and elsewhere. His work is held in the collections of the universities of Colorado and New Mexico, the Herbert Johnson Museum, and others. Mr. Evett painted the large murals in the rotunda of the Nebraska state capitol. He has recently been writing critical pieces published in the *New Republic*.

Mr. Evett is chairman of the Cornell University department of art.

Mr. Evett, I would like for you to discuss your dual role as artist and as teacher. How did you come to university teaching in the first place?

I think it had a lot to do with the fact that I had to support a family and there was no work for an artist. One couldn't make a living. It's commonplace, I guess, that artists don't make a living. At the time that I was ready to start teaching, there were plenty of jobs to be had. I was visiting my dealer in New York and she had a telephone call from the head of the art department here who also exhibited in that gallery, asking if she knew of anybody who could come on short notice to Cornell. So I came up here and liked it and I have been here for about twenty-five years.

I think it was understood by most people in my generation that what we would do to make a living, if we could, was to teach at the college level. This is an idea that is routine now, of course.

You asked me a crucial question right off the bat about the interrelationship between being a teacher and being an artist.

Since I have been at it for twenty-five years, I have some feelings about the subject that certainly would be different from those of a person who was just beginning in the game. When I think about it, I realize that one of the weakest things about college teaching is the provincial position of most art teachers vis-à-vis the New York art scene. Even though I have a gallery in New York, I have never done the New York scene or made any effort, never had any competence at the *business* of being an artist in New York. You have to work at it. In response to the pressures and possibilities of New York art, as that milieu affected university life, I have a feeling that I was not strictly honest in affirming my own convictions. Our students are very sensitive to the dominant mode of American art, which is novelty, as you know. They are constantly aware of the latest thing. A lot of them come from New York City and are fairly sophisticated and they bring some kind of pressure—the sanction that has gone with vanguardism in American art—to bear on their life here. In terms of my own career as a teacher, I think I have been much too permissive and much too responsive in the wrong ways to that kind of pressure.

I remember once going to a College Art Association meeting. A well-known sculptor came and talked to the college art teachers and his air of condescension and arrogance was obvious. He was a real artist who worked at it and I can quite understand why he would sense the difference between his role as a hard-working day-by-day artist and these people who were somewhat compromised. I think the fundamental relationship is one of compromise in teaching and being an artist at the same time. Maybe people who do that are not totally given over to being artists or they wouldn't do it.

Teaching takes a lot out of an artist. I think if he has any integrity as a teacher, any sense of responsibility about what he owes his students, he tries to teach them the best that he knows. He tries to make it as clear as possible. Now somehow when that is given out and sort of regurgitated back, something happens to the vitality of the concept, if there ever was any in it. I guess it also depends on the nature of the teacher, what he is trying to do with students, and again, thinking back over a career of being a teacher, I have come to believe that my teaching in general was wrong. What I tried to do was to get people to paint good pictures according to my concepts of what good pictures were. I think that's an error that many teachers make. They use their students as surrogates for themselves. In a sense, teaching becomes a creative act and you get other people to do what you don't have time and energy to do and you apply your own notions about what constitutes order and clarity or formal beauty or whatever it is. There are two evils there: I think it is not really useful for the student and I think it deprives the artist of some of his creative energy. I think a lot of us doubt that you can teach art and I have often felt as a teacher that there was an inherent incongruity in the whole thing. We can talk about it and maybe if we are really good, we can give someone else a kind of sense of the meaning about the activity itself. But the idea of teaching professional skills seems an absurdity in light of the total decline of standards of professional skill in American art. That hasn't been the game. The game has been the search for idiosyncratic gestures and novelty, and the whole idea of a tradition that is transmitted from one generation to the next, which is what a university tries to do, has had rough going in the face of this strong cultural move in the other direction. That gets back to what I guess I was thinking when I first started talking. Not only is there a kind of fundamental inconsistency in trying to teach art, but the whole idea of artists being in the university is, in some ways, absurd. I don't feel that as much now as I used to but I have plenty of friends here who are scholars and highly trained intellectuals and I sense that they regard an artist in the university as something of an interloper. In some ways I agree with them, because what they have to contribute is of a certain precision and clarity and has a background of tradition and organization that makes it possible for them to function effectively.

This is all very circuitous, but my ideas about teaching in the university have to do with personal experience and a recent change in my idea about what being an artist means. I had been in Spain for not quite a year; I frequently had gone to Europe and painted pictures out-of-doors but never had I done it with such concentration. I worked almost every day, getting up early in the morning, going out to paint outside. It was the simplest kind of procedure, just looking at nature, walking around in that ambience of sights, sounds, winds, and odors, looking for the right place to work, while enjoying everything that has to do with being a human being out-of-doors. Using a process of working in which I have watercolor tablets, one brush, simple paint box, pigments, and water, I begin with one single stroke, just a mark and then another and then another. And there is something about this process that gets one engaged in a rhythm of seeing which goes beyond just the simple act of recording: it becomes almost a mystical experience of being in the presence of nature. You begin to feel that you are there and that you are alive and that what you are doing is an innately good thing. So when I came back to teach last fall, I had the notion that I would no longer try to teach people to paint pretty pictures, or good pictures, or stylish pictures, or anything like that, or even that I would teach them abstract systems. I came to feel that in general, abstract problems were not very useful and that the current emphasis on abstraction was a mistake, that it was debilitating in some way. The fundamental idea that I came back with was that all that counted was that a person be engaged in a process of seeing, responding, and recording, no more, no less, and that that was really what it was all about. Anyway, it turned out to be a very mixed-up year because I had one class of majors, kids who had had good training in high school and who intended to be artists and many of whom had had fairly sophisticated backgrounds and who had already got this thing about making good art, you know, or wanting to be up-to-date. I had another class of students from out of our department who were just interested in drawing from life. Well, it turned out that the ones who were just here to draw (had no idea about making good art or anything like that) were in great harmony with this idea of mine and I worked very well with them and we had a good time, and the atmosphere that they generated was really wonderful—a sense of people engaged in a process that was immediately fulfilling. Whereas with the other class, the whole thing just fell apart—the idea of looking at nature, of trying to make these simple kinds of connections just didn't come about at all with the art majors. I'm still brooding about why that occurred. I'm not quite sure what it was that went wrong. But I am still pretty much convinced there is something in this idea that is valid. It is so simple, God knows, that what really counts is the *moment* of creation, that that's just about all you have and art is that which comes about as a result of someone having this moment of responding and mark-making.

I'm curious whether anyone's going to make any qualitative judgment about this artifact that happened?

That's a good question and it's difficult for me to answer because I have a very strong Presbyterian sense of right and wrong, good and bad. I have looked at a lot of the art of the world. I am devoted to the art of Italy. I have some sense of the grandeur of great art. At least I know there is such a thing. I love European art in general, and therefore, obviously there's the problem of how you relate what you believe to be of lasting value in the art of the past to this other notion of the significance of the process. I have some feeling that as a teacher it may be possible, if you have subtle insights into what constitutes great art, to talk about it using reproductions and slides for reference. If you have some standards that relate to the most significant and deepest levels of the art you are in, you may be able to communicate something of that although I'm not quite sure how it's done. The whole notion of the existence of high art is something that I would like to maintain, at the same time approach it in some other way than I have done in the past, relying somehow on the integrity of this *moment* that I'm talking about as the way to do it. I did some painting in Cezanne's

Provence and Van Gogh's Saint-Rémy, and became even more convinced than I had been before that the secret of their creative power was not abstract thinking but just the intensity of their interest in what was around them, especially in the case of Van Gogh. You know, we have heard so much about his erratic emotional life, whereas in fact, I think as a painter he was just passionately looking and absorbed in the process of finding the appropriate marks to such an intense degree that what came out of it was that vital art. It is something like what I am trying to find, some kinds of conditions where the students can do that unselfconsciously without the interruption of abstract concerns. Does that sound at all clear?

Yes, but I'm still hung up on the standards, I suppose. There must have been others who looked at this scenery with as much passion as Van Gogh. What is the difference?

It may sound awfully sly but I suspect that the difference is in the intensity of the emotion of the observer; that in this mode of working, where you are concentrating on the process rather than the product, the value thing (which God knows is almost impossible to pin down) would subtly be related to the intensity of the observation, and maybe some mysterious thing like talent. But I am now thinking as far as education is concerned that I would be willing to see mounds of art work, mountains of it, produced by people (even though it does suggest an ecological problem) in this creative action, and I am somehow convinced of the validity of this process in the university as I never was before. As I say, I always felt slightly uncomfortable about having the title of professor in a university because I recognized I didn't have scholarly training. And now I have the feeling because of the way society has changed and other factors, that these experiences in art—and I'm talking about the experiences, not the product—that these are innately good. Good for students and good for human life and as an educational process, innately good. That kind of immediacy is something that is essential to an educated person's existence and happiness. I now tend to feel that those ideas that Herbert Read offered in his book called *Redemption of the Robot*, which seemed at first glance to be kind of ridiculous, are not. His idea is that education in the arts is fundamental to any education and fundamental to the development of healthy psyches. I am willing to go along with that, simply because in the nature of this process of organizing, releasing, and fulfilling, even though it's only for an hour or two a day, there is something in that which is wholesome and constructive.

So we are coming full circle. You began by saying that in certain ways you felt the notion of an artist in the university was absurd, but now, because of this new revelation, you're more convinced of the validity of your work here. Your process is just as good as the botanist's.

Right. I'll say more than that. I don't even want to compare it in terms of good and bad. I just think it is something that is needed. Needed at all levels of education but needed very much at the university level also. I think an interesting, enriching thing can happen if you bring to the university artists who are reasonably intelligent, sensitive, and articulate about their role as artists. We have a person who's teaching here now who is supremely articulate and sensitive and subtle, a really great teacher. What he does for his students, I think, goes way beyond the ordinary kind of teaching.

There are some obvious rewards in this profession. We lead markedly good lives. University people do, as you know. We are reasonably well paid and we have ample time. It's been possible for me to go abroad fairly regularly because I have had sabbatical leaves and free summers. My children have been brought up in a very stimulating and interesting environment, so the satisfactions that have to do with conventional middle-class joys are obvious. Accompanying that are also the corrupting things that have to do with solid middle-class joys. The lack of connection with the real world and living at a level of privilege that is special compared to the way most people live means that you really don't have any idea of what real life is like after a number of years in this kind of environment.

I must say, I don't think that I have produced any great artists, that any of my students have turned out to be professional successes (whatever that means in this day and age). In general, I have a feeling that I've not been a good teacher. Once in a while I have some sense that I have been able to reach a student and have been useful. I am now fifty-seven and I see things in a slightly different perspective. Fifty-seven is not a cheerful time in life.

Generally, do you like to teach?

I'm not sure that I do. I think it's just about 50/50. I do and I don't.

So you like to teach maybe 50 percent of the time; what's wrong with the other 50 percent?

I guess it has to do with a feeling of lack of connection with my students for some reason, and it's really remarkable how these rhythms vary. Sometimes you get a group of people with whom you have rapport and the whole thing seems to move well, and other times you get off on the wrong foot, something goes wrong and that thing seems to be shot to hell. It's when you have that feeling of not being in rapport with your class that the 50 percent bad feeling occurs.

How do you define "not being in rapport with your class"? How can you tell whether you have any rapport with them or not?

I think attendance is an obvious factor. If they don't come, you can be pretty sure they are not interested. The measure I would consider would be the intensity with which they work. If they don't seem interested in working, then I have a feeling that I haven't done what I'm supposed to do as a teacher. I recognize one of the obstacles in this whole thing is the egocentricity of artists (God knows I wish I could get out of that) and the egocentricity of teachers. I think many artists feel that they are laying themselves on the line when they teach, and if they are not welcomed as teachers and the students don't respond, they feel rejected. That's a curious thing. On the whole, I really don't like most artists, when I think about it. We have had a program here for years of inviting people up from New York to conduct seminars and things like that. They are only here for a short period of time and 90 percent of those people seemed to me like monsters—particularly those who live in New York and have played that New York game for years, where you are out to get people, out to survive and make the right maneuvers, and you don't really consider people as people but as pawns in your game of operating on the scene.

I suspect that people who teach in universities and who for any reason blame university teaching for their lack of success as artists are hypocrites. I suspect that people who teach in universities are not all that intense as artists or they wouldn't be willing to divide their time to that extent. I really think that there is something in Shaw's remark about "Those who can, do; those who can't, teach."

Well, I would not have been interested in coming to talk with you if you hadn't been active as a painter. You continue to work, do you not?

Sometimes. Art is largely a matter of habit. If you are in the habit of getting up every day and working, then you're an artist. I think an artist is somebody who is so compulsively busy with this one form of activity that he doesn't have time to do anything else. And I know damn well that in a subtle way I use being on committees involved in university business as a delaying tactic. What I am saying is, I use these diversions as an excuse for not working. Unless you are in the habit of it, working is very difficult. And I think the rhythm of university teaching is a real obstacle. This is an obstacle for the students as well as for the faculty. If an artist has classes, for example, on Monday, Wednesday, and Friday, and he tries to paint on Tuesday, Thursday, and Saturday, it takes a certain amount of energy to get going each day. Everybody knows that beginning to face up to aesthetic decisions which often are complex and difficult isn't an easy thing to do. Therefore, if you have some nice excuse such as being on a committee or whatever, it's easy enough to let the painting go by the board. I have done very little this winter.

Did you have these feelings ten years ago about the difference between the real "dirty-hands" artist and the rather safe "squeaky-clean" university artist?

No I didn't. The people who used to come up here during the days of abstract expressionism were semiliterate, crude, deliberately foul-mouthed; they sort of grunted. The thought of these arrogant bastards coming up here and grunting at a university audience struck me as ridiculous. There was a visiting critic who came up here and absolutely shattered his class. He had them doing things that they thought were wonderful fun for two or three months and then they suddenly found out that they were just being tools for this guy, he was using them for experiments of his own devising, and they just all of a sudden gave up on it altogether and it took a long time for those kids to pull themselves together again. Many of them quit school because there seemed to be nothing left for them with any meaning. That kind of thing can be very upsetting.

I am wondering whether or not you think it's absolutely necessary for creative personalities like you who come to the university to teach to have a circle of like-minded professionals, a certain critical mass of that kind of talent? Is that necessary for your own productivity, your own happiness?

I don't know how many one needs but I think a teacher needs some kind of support somewhere in the department; one or two people are enough. I see the necessity of having a group of like-minded colleagues even though their work may be quite different; I think that is essential if you're going to function. I also think in an ideal department you should have a great diversity of views, and somehow people should learn to live together in spite of disagreements on aesthetics and practical problems of running the department.

There's another way of answering the question. Could you ever be engaged as artist-in-residence in some small college?

If it were an artist-in-residence sort of thing, I think I would seriously consider it because I have always felt that one of the weaknesses of teaching in the university is that the artists don't contribute sufficiently to the life of the university in the way that they can contribute best. They don't produce work for the university. If I had my way, I would see that part of the requirement of an artist's tenure in a university would be to make a contribution in terms of what he paints as well as his teaching. If he is half artist and half teacher, I think he really ought to be half artist. I used to have a plan in which all resident artists would be expected to spend half their time producing for the university. I really like the idea of commissioned work. If people got into the habit of working for some purpose, the fact that it would be a strictly local kind of display would seem wholesome to me rather than not.

After all, it's an educated citizenry you're working for.

Exactly. It would have to do with making an environment in which the arts are constantly visible. There are plenty of empty wall surfaces. Even though much of the work would not be of any lasting value, I think it should be turned over to the university and I actually think that universities could build up quite interesting collections if they used all the artists who had ever worked there. If they left this contribution as part of life there, it would be a good thing, I think. I've never been able to implement this notion.

What do you think has happened to your own creative output in terms of both quality and quantity as a result of your affiliation with a university?

If I could separate this notion of novelty and newness in the whole American art world from teaching, that might be helpful, but I don't see how I could. They're related.

I don't understand what you mean.

63   KENNETH EVETT

The thing that I am talking about is the effect of the art magazines, the art establishment, on teaching. It's a very important effect, particularly at a certain period in one's life. When one reads art magazines, one knows what the latest thing is. Now the effect of this preoccupation with the latest thing (so typical of American life in general) has for me been insidiously bad. Partly in order to maintain some kind of contact with the students and to be respected by them, I have tried to be more permissive and more accepting of various new modes than my real convictions would lead me to be. And to the degree that that was dishonest, I think it was bad, and to the degree that university teachers accept this provincial role, the less they are likely to affirm their own beliefs.

You've felt constrained to do something or try to be something because you are a professor of art that you would not have felt if you had been a loner? We were talking about your work *and you were saying what happened to you in* teaching. *Did that also limit your own output?*

It did indeed. Now whether what I have been describing is just a hindsight view of one's life and career, I'm not sure. What I am saying is that as a teacher and as an artist, I have been much too accepting—I won't say "aware" because I'm not sure I have been aware—I have been somehow too responsive to the pressures exerted by the art scene in this country. As a teacher and as a painter, I wish I had had more strength of character, more firmness, more conviction about my own vision than I had.

But now that you can say that, where do you go from here?

I'm now of a mind to be more independent, both as a teacher and as a painter, than I ever was before in my life. That gets back to this vision on the road to Madrid or wherever it occurred.

Suppose for a minute I am trying to get you away from Cornell. What would a department have to provide for it to be your ideal situation?

I have already described it. I would have it demand of me that I function as an artist as well as a teacher in equal parts. That would be *the* job. I notice one thing that happens to artists in this society is that they are sort of used up and cast aside. You know how rapidly things change in the art game. I have always admired a discipline of the Renaissance: working for a particular place. The intellectual problems involved in commissioned work of that kind have always intrigued me, and in general working within the framework of requirements appeals to me because, as I have indicated, it demands a certain kind of imagination. As far as the teaching is concerned, I believe in having a student body that consists of non-artists and artists. We now have it worked out so that in our classes we will have architects, art majors, and students from outside the department. We hope there will be a kind of leavening among people with different capacities. Hopefully, something good will happen with this amalgam.

Why does that appeal to you?
In some says it gets away from this awful egocentricity that artists suffer from. Some students who come here are all hung up on a self-centered concern with their little mark and how important it is to maintain their egos. Well, maybe that's part of their youth; they're holding onto their sense of self as desperately as they can. Maybe they have to do that. In the classes that I think are good, the atmosphere is not self-centered. It is oriented, focused on something outside one's self, in the process of relating to (particularly in the case of life drawing) a human being—trying to make marks that are expressive of the abstract unities and vital essence of another human being.

What is it you and your colleagues in the department of art at Cornell try to do for students?
We don't know, of course. When I think about our department and all the individuals in it, each one has a different idea about what he wants to do. We have no shared notion about what we want to do. We have independence and I think that's

one of the strengths of Cornell as a university. It's always been willing to have people come here who were idiosyncratic and who were encouraged to do whatever it was they did without anybody bothering them. That kind of independence I'm sure is characteristic of most good schools.

I don't think it's possible in this country to have an integrated art program. I can't conceive of it working. There isn't any shared understanding about what it is people are trying to do. I also have a feeling that what students want, in spite of what we think they want, is some kind of stable exposure to certain kinds of fundamentals (if there are such things). I think students really want to know about technique. It's kind of an interim thing; it's not really art. But to have a good technique is reliable. Therefore, I have some feeling that good art schools in the near future will be having more courses that have to do with traditional techniques and processes that are workable, where the student has some feeling of competence and control.

We have a student here now who wants to be a great painter in a traditional way, with glazes and solid drawing, the whole shebang. He wants to be a great artist and has no interest in anything else. I wish him well.

What would you change about your department tomorrow if you had a chance?

Nothing. Oddly enough, nothing. I'd have to work hard to think of things about it that seem to me restrictive or bad or moving in the wrong direction.

Have you any other dissatisfactions with university life other than those we have discussed?

No, I'm afraid I don't. I like the life, as I have mentioned. I think it's probably too soft, but I have to confess that it's enjoyable.

Are you happy?

Sometimes. I have many moments of real joy and those are mostly related to my painting. Without those days to enjoy, then I guess I'm not. I have to find some means whereby I can do in the winter, while I'm teaching, something comparable to what I do in the summer, when I'm not teaching: set up this rhythm of day-by-day work. That's pretty difficult, and in a sense that is the dilemma for the artist-teacher.

Carroll Glenn

Carroll Glenn was born in Richmond, Virginia, October 28, 1924.
She studied at the Juilliard School with Edouard Dethier and
later with Ivan Galamian. At age sixteen she made her New York
Town Hall debut. At eighteen she appeared with both the New
York Philharmonic and the Philadelphia Orchestra. By age
twenty-one she had won the Schubert Memorial, the National
Foundation of Music Clubs Young Artist Award, the Naumburg
Award, and the Town Hall Award. Since then she has appeared
as recitalist and soloist with orchestras throughout the United
States, Canada, Mexico, South America, Europe, and Asia.
She is a specialist in the little-known violin music of Liszt and
Richard Strauss, early Italian concerti, and she has played pre-
mieres of works by Andrew Imbrie, Gail Kubik, Harold Morris,
and Anis Fuleihan, much of which repertory is recorded on Co-
lumbia, Westminster, Turnabout, and other labels.

Eugene List

Eugene List was born in Philadelphia July 6, 1918. At age ten he
appeared as soloist with the Los Angeles Philharmonic. He was a
student of Olga Samaroff at the Philadelphia Conservatory and at
the Juilliard School in New York City.

He played the first New York City performance of the Shosta-
kovich Piano Concerto No. 1 with the New York Philharmonic in
1935. During that year his Town Hall debut occurred. Since then
Mr. List has appeared as recitalist and soloist with orchestras on
all continents.

A highlight of Mr. List's career was a performance he gave in
1945 at the Potsdam Conference, where he played for President
Truman, Prime Minister Churchill, and General Stalin.

Mr. List has recorded repertory ranging from Mozart through

Chávez for Columbia, Mercury, Vanguard, Vox, and other companies.

Carroll Glenn and Eugene List are married and appear together in concerts and recordings. They both taught at the Eastman School of Music, University of Rochester, and since 1975 they have lived and taught in New York City.

How did you two happen to become faculty members?

GLENN

Eugene always says that so many things happen by chance. One of the big examples of that was when he was in the service and played at Potsdam, which was just a chance thing, and it was wonderful for him when he came out of the service. The telephone just rang one night and it was Dean Cuthbert at North Texas. He told me of the tragedy of Marjorie Fulton's having been killed and asked if I would come. I said I couldn't come at that time but if he would call back in a few days we would think about it. Our children had gotten over babyhood. Both of our parents had helped us so much with them when they were small and we had traveled. We thought that when they got older, it would be no problem. It's only when you have children that you realize that late childhood and the teens are really the tricky part to bringing them up. I was finding it more and more difficult to be away from them and yet I had always been so active, I didn't want to just stop and stay home. And so when he called, it was just sort of the catalytic force that set our thoughts into motion. I remember going upstairs and talking to Allison and asking her if she wanted to go live where the cowboys were. She had never cared for New York and so she was greatly in accord and that's how we went there.

Eugene did a big Russian tour that year so he wasn't there too much, but when he was there, they were very fond of him. Dean Cuthbert tried several times to get him on the North Texas faculty. He had been approached by Texas Christian University, and if we had stayed there he probably would have gone to T.C.U.

LIST

I probably would because T.C.U. is so close and we could
have remained in Denton. It seemed very interesting to me. By
this time I had gotten interested in the whole thing through
Carroll and through the people we met there. The move was already in that direction. So many people we admired had gone
into teaching and kept up their playing. What we always hoped
was that we could do both so that, in a way, we could have the
best of both worlds, you might say.

*Were you living in New York at the time, both concertizing but not
teaching at all?*

LIST

A little coaching perhaps, but not a formal affiliation. Things
just hadn't moved in that direction. We were fortunate in that
two positions opened simultaneously at Eastman; that's rather
unusual, you know.

The school at that time was very interested and very open to
the idea of concerts; they liked the idea that members of the faculty be active and travel. It's good for us; it's good for them. I
think the school was also entering a stage where they wanted to
emphasize a little more the applied music. The school had
always been famous for its composers and for theory and for
many other things. They were strong in many areas and they
had outstanding people here but I think they wanted to emphasize it a little bit more by bringing in people who not only
taught but who did play.

*You haven't felt pressures to be in the studio Monday, Tuesday, and
Thursday every week, nine months out of the year?*

LIST

They are very flexible; they want you to give the lessons to
which the students are entitled but we can make our own programs. If we want to teach just evenings, I suppose theoretically

we could. We try to fit into the regular schedule. Of course the first year it wasn't possible because the concerts are always arranged at least a year in advance, so we came in with certain things that were already fixed. But after that we realized that you can't just go away for six weeks and have the students floundering around. So then we told our management that we didn't want to be away for weeks on end because it would not be good for the students; it would not be good for the school.

I'm curious about what kinds of feelings you both have about teaching—when you (rather late in a career by ordinary standards) realized that you would be in a studio teaching.

LIST

I think it presents a great challenge. (I suppose that's a remark that is made very frequently.) It's a formidable challenge and you feel that these students are in a way your musical children and they are in your hands during this period and you have that kind of responsibility. You take pride and happiness in their achievement. You try to guide them and point things out, which you can do from the point of view of your experience. Everyone says this but I never realized it until I did it myself. Everyone says, "But it's so good for me; I have learned so much through teaching." And you think, "Yes, yes, of course," but you *really* do. You learn an awful lot.

We've been taught by our own teachers, of course, and the aim of all teaching, after all, is to make the student independent so that the student will eventually stand on his own. So then you go off and you start playing your own concerts and touring and all that, and when you have a new piece to learn, you sit down and learn it. I mean you have been given certain musical tools, procedures, techniques, and so you work and you're not asking yourself questions all the time. But the students will come in and you have to be able to translate your ideas into things that will really register with the students. You can't just say, "Well, do it this way." You have to say, "This is a musical phrase" (to take something very obvious); "the phrase has a high point, the phrase has a low point, it goes to this point, that's the point of greatest intensity." You have to begin to crystalize your own musical thoughts. In that way students are extremely interesting and they really force you to think about music—what you are doing technically, musically, emotionally. Why is one style different from another? What makes it different? It's an education (which is I know a very trite thing to say). Because you finally come to grips with a certain aesthetic that is not just sitting down and wiggling your fingers, then it reflects in your playing. I think it strengthens your playing and I think this is true with most people. At least that has been my experience. I think there is a very valuable interplay. Hopefully we are helping the students (which of course is our main concern), but we get a very valuable spin-off from this ourselves.

GLENN

We've talked about these things at home to the point where, because of our poor kids, we finally had to stop it. But you do become fascinated. Another thing that I appreciate very much in a university atmosphere and music school the caliber of Eastman is the serious atmosphere. I mean, you remember how you were when you heard the Franck Symphony for the first time; well, these kids are beyond that, but the sense of wonder at the discovery of music is ever present. Also, they are young enough so they are not that practical and they despise anything commercial. When you have been touring for quite a few years, you have to think about what an audience will react to. Students don't care. You say something about "This is good for the audience," and they look at you as if you were from another world. It may be even more with this generation of students because they don't care for appearance at all. You are constantly immersed in a serious musical atmosphere instead of a commercial one. There's nothing wrong with the commercial one; it's fine, but that seriousness is a very charming thing to have around you all the time.

LIST

I think another thing that is fascinating for us is the psychological aspect: you realize very early in the game that every student is an individual. But then you realize that there is a way of applying a successful technique and approach to students even though they are very different and you have to approach them differently.

It sounds to me as if neither of you were afraid to teach. It was just kind of a new adventure.

LIST

Well, I think it's also a change in concept. When we were first playing, it was almost the kiss of death as far as management was concerned. If you went out and taught somewhere, then management more or less wrote you off. But good positions are now greatly sought after and it is considered a very fine thing. Think of the outstanding Russian artists who teach, the outstanding European artists who teach.

GLENN

That has gradually changed. I think Gyorgy Sandor was one of the first who began to change this opinion, and now managements are delighted because it takes a certain amount of pressure off them; they really appreciate it now.

LIST

A person like Gyorgy is able to arrange his life so that he does play concerts. He records. We try to arrange our life so we can too. We discovered shortly after we came here that January was a good month to be away for instance, because there were finals. I have recorded very often at Christmastime because nothing was going on here so I wasn't missing anything. You try to fit it into certain parts of your schedule where you know the demands aren't very great.

One of the things I noticed when I started was that suddenly you have a family of twenty young people. I don't know if other people react that way, but it is a large family of people you feel responsible for. I don't mean that they are living in your house, but you are responsible for them, and to take on that kind of thing with that number of people, I found that there was an adjustment necessary. Once you adjust to it, you realize that's the way it is and it seems perfectly normal after that. You arrange for your practice time, you arrange for your teaching time, you arrange for your "being away time" and your playing time. But when you first cope with it, you have the feeling of needing time all the time.

GLENN

I think you always cope with it.

Is that a big problem for you?

LIST

I think yes. I think budgeting time is a big problem, because when we are very busy, it means that we try to save certain parts of the day for ourselves. Then no matter what happens the rest of the day, we feel that that part of the day has been taken care of. But in a very busy time, if you have deadlines ahead of you, you have to budget time, plan it, and even so the day just stretches out for too long sometimes.

GLENN

Of course, we have always practiced till midnight. It just makes an occupied life, I think. When you are a student, all you do is practice. Then you get married and you practice and then you have children and you are married and you practice. And at our stage we are married and practice and have children and have students so it becomes more complicated, but you get better able to cope with it too. This year we have been fortunate because we have gotten a reduction in hours, which I think is a very nice step. I think universities could explore with great profit the system of using assistants. I think eventually that would be a very helpful thing.

Am I wrong in understanding that you took your first academic position mainly because of your children and your home life or were there other factors?

GLENN

Well, the concert picture changed quite a lot in the United States. As you know, group attractions came in and I think there were fewer recitals. If you look at a concert list anywhere, you see a ballet company, an orchestra, Emil Gilels or Artur Rubinstein or a Russian folk group. There will be one recital. When we began to play, there would be a violinist, a pianist, a male singer, and a female singer, you know, and once in a great while they would have a trio or something like that.

LIST

I think it has to do with the fact that you can send a ballet company all over the world today. It may be expensive but it's possible, because they will fly, say, from Stuttgart or from Moscow and they will rehearse for a week in New York and then they will put on a season and they will move around in the country and their government subsidizes them to some degree. If people see the Ballet Russe or whatever it is on Ed Sullivan, they will say, "Oh, we must have this in our town." Well, I don't blame them but it has changed the picture very much; it's now the big picture and the big sound, and a soloist doesn't have the bigness or richness of sound of a symphony orchestra. The interesting thing, though, was that before, the two existed quite happily together.

GLENN

And then another thing. Now, I think, one would want to do it for status, because now many people of great prominence have accepted university positions of some sort or another—the better positions in particular. They are greatly sought after. People who are playing all the time are also at universities. So the whole picture has changed, and you would feel a little bit out of it if you weren't teaching, I think.

LIST

Another thing that strikes me is that it is very hard to be sensational anymore because the level is so high. We were talking with Francescatti about this once.

Maybe the recital picture has become a dull picture. We may be responsible for preserving something that maybe shouldn't be preserved. How exciting is it? Somebody in black and white bows and sits down and plays and then stands up and bows and walks off. Is that spectacle? Is that something that grips an audience, is that something that gets them all worked up? Before people were exposed to many different experiences of all kinds, I think probably a recital was a very exciting and satisfying event. If you were in a small town anywhere and a visiting artist came to town, that was probably a terrific event. It's hard for us to put ourselves back in time. Now we are saturated. I think that it has become less and less a dazzling event.

GLENN

Francescatti said when he came and played the Paganini Concerto here the first time, he made a tremendous success—which he did. I remember. And of course he is a great artist anyhow, but he said now every kid in Mr. Galamian's class plays the Paganini Concerto marvelously, you know.

Let's talk some more about what life is like in a university.

LIST

I am involved in some meetings and I am always amazed at how much time it takes, and even when something is decided, at how long it takes to implement it. Finally one becomes discouraged. The system takes hours and hours of time when you are sitting in committees. Committee work is very slow, whereas if one person is setting policy, he can decide in five minutes if he's going to have this or if he's going to have that. I'm sure you must get discouraged with committee meetings. I think everybody does. Our daughter went to a new college where the students were supposed to participate with the teachers and the administration. Well, very few of the students participated.

Why? Were they just bored with the whole idea?

LIST

Well, many of them are really not qualified. They may give ideas but do they really know how to run a big organization? And a lot of them are not interested. They think they are interested. They love to sit in and tell the teachers and administration what to do and I really think that they should be brought in. The first meeting is exciting and you get a lot of razzmatazz going, but you know, if you have to sit for twenty-five meetings how many people still have the tenacity and the enthusiasm to stick it through, whereas the administration knows it has to. I mean they have to finally decide what policy is going to be.

GLENN

When we first were involved with this, we used to think that the professors would know exactly what to do, and I think in a way we have more respect for administration now because we realize that it's not that simple a thing and requires a firm hand. Somebody has to hold the line. You get this spirited faculty and equally spirited student body and somebody has to hold things tight. It's not that you agree with every decision 100 percent, but you do develop a lot more respect for the job itself. We have learned a lot during the seven years we've been here.

You two haven't griped at all. I am wondering what two gifted artists who are involved here find most frustrating?

GLENN

Time.

Time is number one, huh?

GLENN

I would say so.

LIST

Yes. I would say that's one of the main things. There's not too much that can be done about that. You can cut down the number of hours, of course. That would be ideal. I think part of it, too, is that there is sometimes not enough screening of students, so that some students come in who perhaps shouldn't be in the school at all. People do turn up at your studio after the beginning of the year who are really poorly equipped and you feel they shouldn't be there. It's not only that it's uninteresting from our point of view, but they are going to have a terrible awakening sometime when they step out into the outside world where people are going to tell them in a brutal way, "You're not a pianist, you're not a violinist, you're not a singer." This isn't just our school; it's everywhere.

What if I were trying to get you away from Eastman to come to my school to teach, what would that school need?

LIST

Well, I would think not too heavy a schedule. We both came to that.

GLENN

I was thinking of this because we are so active playing.

LIST

I think it's forced us to look at time. It is time and salary and the freedom to go off and play. I think those are the three things that interest us.

GLENN

And caliber of students—appropriate talent. For example, it's silly for Eugene to be teaching three-octave scales to students for the first time. That's a misplacement; it's a mismatching. He should be matched with appropriate students. I would like the same thing.

Do you feel that your own artistic careers, professional careers, have been changed in any profound way by your affiliation with the Eastman School?

LIST

I don't think so.

GLENN

I think they have been changed more by the general changing picture. I think that the picture is just very different than when we started to do most of our playing.

LIST

We feel this makes it increasingly difficult for the young people coming up today unless there is something fantastic. How many Van Cliburns are there going to be who win in Moscow? That was an extraordinary event. Once he did that, it was so spectacular that the man in the street knew about it and it led to a big career.

GLENN

One thing that has changed in our lives is the fact that you have a tremendously rich musical experience. For example, if you teach, say, twenty to twenty-five hours a week, you are forcibly immersed 100 percent in great composers. Your mind is working on music: Brahms, Beethoven, Bartók, always something very interesting and your mind goes to work on that.

LIST

I think from that point of view it keeps you in a much wider repertory. At the beginning, I think it is a strain because you are not accustomed to this kind of thing. You know yourself that you couldn't be handling all that music yourself during any one given week. There would be no reason to. It's a curious thing, because our craft or whatever you want to call it is to play everything as beautifully as possible, which in itself limits. You know, if you have everything up to a kind of mediocre level and say, "Well, I just want to know a lot of music," you explore a lot of music but that's something else. Who wants to hear music played at that level?

GLENN

The artist has to be able to endure this kind of tremendous discipline: going after the last little detail. The difference between the sight reader and the artist is partly this. Maybe it's even a limitation of the personality of the artist, but that's what being an artist implies.

LIST

The student finds it very hard at the end to go up that last inch or two. They have already done a tremendous amount of work and it's really sounding quite good, but it doesn't have anything distinctive or extraordinary. It's not sensational. They find it very hard. It's hard for everybody and that's sort of the inch that kills, and a lot of it is just sheer drudgery. They would like to feel that you sit down at the piano and you enjoy it all. Well, you enjoy a great deal of it, but you don't enjoy it all.

James Hendricks

James Hendricks was born in Little Rock, Arkansas, August 7, 1938. He studied at the universities of Arkansas (B.A.) and Iowa (M.F.A.).

Notable among showings of his paintings are several one-man exhibitions, including one at the Smithsonian Institution, and exhibitions at the National Gallery of Art and the San Francisco Museum of Art. His work is held in collections of the Smithsonian, the National Gallery (a commission), and elsewhere—especially in the Northeast.

Mr. Hendricks teaches at the University of Massachusetts.

Mr. Hendricks, how were you drawn to a faculty position?

Purely economic reasons. I like teaching; I wouldn't do it if I didn't like it. I would get out and do something else. My wife's family and some members of my family are teachers and they like it, so I knew something about teaching. I was willing to give it a chance and it worked out very well.

What's been satisfying about it?

The fact that I've discovered I can do my own creative work and teach at the same time. The teaching profession (at the college level) allows time; the teaching load is not so heavy that there isn't plenty of time left for work. It's gradually evolved, and the longer I teach the more I'm able to utilize my time more efficiently and get my work done. One of the reasons I like being here is because it is close to New York City (which is the main art scene of the world), and I can get in there from time to time and see all the exhibitions I want to see. In fact I go to New York on the average of once a month.

You say you enjoy teaching. Why?

I am stimulated by the students and by seeing students grow and develop their creative ideas and make a success of, say, a

B.F.A. major in art and go on into professional work; this is a satisfying thing. I myself have improved in my understanding of art by watching the students solve problems and discover art for themselves. It's difficult to say why I like it so much. I really do like teaching though.

Do you think you enjoy seeing students develop from a human point of view or from a professional point of view?

It's difficult to see any professional development in an undergraduate; you can see them going in that direction, but it'll probably be several years before they'll be doing professional-level work. It's not that so much; it's just discovering themselves, and what they're happy doing.

It's probably in my background: I started as a zoology major. In fact, I was in geology and engineering, and finally in zoology; I finished my undergraduate degree in zoology. But I took electives in art and more and more became involved in art during the science degree and really discovered what I was happy doing—what I really enjoyed doing—and discovered myself that way.

That's a very satisfying thing to know—that other people are doing it too. Most of our majors have been transfers from other areas. Very few people know that they want to become painters when they get out of high school.

I have an idea (correct me if I'm mistaken) that artist-teachers in the visual arts are not terribly concerned about early technical training.

That's right. Matisse was very late in becoming an active painter; he was in his middle or late thirties before he made his real contribution in painting. Cézanne was late too; he trained in another area.

What, then, are your views about undergraduate training at this school? Do you believe in an "art academy" approach or a more general, liberal education for your students?

I think it has to be both. We should strive for professional standards. As artists, I think we set an example more than anything else if we're active in the studio.

That's the main teaching instrument, really—example. A professional example; someone who is committed to his work, and is producing. That is an educational experience in itself.

What's the example: the product of all this activity, or the activity itself?

The fact that a student sees a faculty member who is committed to producing art, and the fact that the university thinks the artist is important enough to have him around and pay him and give him a studio, and encourage him to produce work.

It's the activity then?

Then students can see how he works, that he is serious about making paintings, and see how he goes about making them. It's the example set. It's one of the main ways of teaching. How he struggles in the studio and makes mistakes, becomes frustrated with failure, and at times is ecstatic with success.

What else do you like about being an artist-teacher in a university?

The main thing is financial support. (There is very little financial support in the arts anywhere except for a very select handful.) It is security that I can have a family; I can live like a decent human being with a decent amount of respect. I can feel that I'm making a contribution in teaching and at the same time carry on my own creative work. I also like the fact that they provide me with an adequate studio with lighting. I've had it for several years now and it's been invaluable. I'm left completely alone to do exactly what I want to do, to pursue any line or style or motif.

What's bugged you about being in a university?

The worst burden to carry in this job is the departmental political activity. This is a very ticklish thing.

Can you afford not to get involved?

Well, it would be very difficult not to be involved. It goes back to what I like about the job: the stability, the income, the opportunity to raise a family. It goes right to the heart of the matter—the reason you're teaching. It's a hierarchy of raises, promotions, success, and so forth.

What other things have bugged you?

Four or five years ago, I would have said that the pressure to publish was a big handicap.

By "publish" you mean exhibit?

Yes. When I graduated from school I was working tremendously in the studio and producing works and not having any success. I had no national juried show until about four years ago. Suddenly, everything began to happen.

Well, artificially contrived pressure by our department in the university situation was a real stimulating factor in getting me off my ass and working. So now I'm really producing, I'm doing shows, and I'm succeeding.

I believe in the value of professional activity; it's what keeps you alive and active. What basis does any instructor have for communicating to a group of painting students, telling them, "This is how to paint!" and giving them criticism when they have had no success creatively or professionally? They have no basis for teaching anything to a group of students unless they are active making drawings and paintings.

Why? I can imagine a man walking into a studio and saying, "This is the way it is." Maybe he's misguided and egocentric, or perhaps he actually is possessed of impeccable taste.

Well then, the next question is, "Who says that's the way it is?" Then I'll say, "I've had success: I've had a high critical opinion of my work. I've been in competition with a hundred other painters and I won the prize. Therefore, my judgment is more accurate than the other hundred." Now of course you can question the critic or the jury. But at least it means you have been active more intensely and have a little more understanding of what it's all about.

What would I have to do to hire you away from here?

The ideal situation would be a nice large studio space. That would be one of the first requirements. Also a teaching load that's not too high (twelve hours a week at the most). There would be very little committee work to be done. This would be the ideal, utopian thing.

Utopia for you doesn't include "no contact with students"?

No. Absolutely not. Most artists I know would probably like to teach some. The biggest fear they have is that it would absorb too much time and too much mental friction. If they're selling for $20,000 a canvas, you know, they don't want to give up too much of their time. They're struggling with their work.

How has your own artistic output been affected by university affiliation?

It's almost as if I as an individual was given a job, a salary, studio space, materials with which to work, and sheltered, nurtured, until I could stand, produce, participate in the arts professionally. That's almost what happened—not by plan but by luck and lots of hard work. Because of these things, I survived (in the process getting tenure, getting a decent salary). But the university does provide this umbrella, you might say.

In other words, I can be totally involved as an artist, and still function in this situation; that's the best thing.

In a way, then, you're saying the university made the whole thing possible.

Yes. Absolutely. I don't think I would have achieved the level of work I'm doing now had I not been in this environment, I really don't.

Walter Kamys

Walter Kamys was born in Chicago June 8, 1917, and studied
there at the Art Institute, as well as in Mexico with Gordon
Onslow-Ford. In 1942 he received the Prix de Rome.

His paintings have been shown in numerous one-man exhibitions in the United States and Europe. They have also appeared
in important exhibits at the Art Institute of Chicago, the Pennsylvania Academy, the Museum of Modern Art, and many
others.

Mr. Kamys teaches at the University of Massachusetts.

I'd like to know how it was you became a teacher?

I'd taught before I came to the university at a series of
schools—art schools, museum schools, and this was kind of a
fluke that I became involved in. I had a show in New York and
it was very successful. The chairman became aware of it and he
contacted me: an emergency had arisen, and he wanted to
know if I would come in and do a stint for one semester. In spite
of the fact that my wife was very much against the idea (she
thought there would be conflict between teaching and my
painting), I decided that since I'd done other types of teaching,
including university extension courses (most of my living had
come in a peripheral way from teaching), that this would give
me an added experience. So I took it and little by little I was just
sucked into it.

*Why did you take it (aside from the things already mentioned)? Did
money have anything to do with it?*

No, not at that particular point; it had nothing to do with it. I
never even asked how much I was going to make. I just took it
because I thought it was a challenge. I wanted to see the type of
students I had to work with, the type of assignment I would
give them and the response I would get from them, and the
response from me. I just wondered. And to this day I say to my

students on the first day of class, "What will you teach me?"

You were just sort of intrigued with the whole idea?
   Oh yes.

What have you enjoyed (or not enjoyed) about being here?
   Well, I think that (just off the top of my head) I like everything about it that I dislike about it.
   I liked the fact that I could relate and become involved with
members of the faculty in other areas. For instance, each day I
look forward to coming into my office because I run into someone from the German department, English department: I can
discuss literature. I never had this opportunity before. I could
practice my Spanish. In fact, even my English is being corrected
by people in the English department. I found this very exciting—this kind of ambience and this kind of relationship. They
themselves were just as intrigued with me as I was with them.
And this is really very exciting.
   Then, too, each semester I discovered that I had a whole new
group of students—until suddenly, I realized that they're all the
same: they look alike, they sound alike, and they have the same
problems. Maybe I'm getting tired of the whole scene, and the
excitement has left me, and there's no more adventure left in it.
But I'm still involved.
   I've never taught summer school before. This is the first year
in the ten years I've been here that I've taught summer school.
And I couldn't sleep all night long thinking about it. I mean I
was still excited by the thought that, "Well, today is the first
class." And what happens to me usually on my first day is I
forget everything. In a day or two, things will calm down for me
and I'll be able to take hold and become immersed, involved,
and then maybe submerged, and it'll be a grind and exciting—
it's just like everything else.

What are you so excited about on your first day of class?
   The first day of anything! I'm excited by getting up in the
morning; I'm excited to see the daylight and to see what this

day will bring because it's the start of a whole new thing for me. It's like starting a new painting. The reason I paint is because I can't wait until I finish it so I can start a new one. It's a whole new beginning again.

Maybe there's something wrong in my psychological makeup. In spite of what I've said about students, yet I'm waiting for that element of surprise. Maybe something will happen that hasn't happened in the past—kind of an eternal hope in mankind. I'm looking in their faces for some aspect of excitement, of stimulus, of some positiveness.

Do you think they sense that search on your part?

Frankly, I have no idea of what they sense in me. All I know is that the students will tell me at some point or another that I'm an exciting teacher, or an unusual teacher.

Some time ago there was some talk about "pot parties," you know. I'd heard this several times over several weeks, and so I finally said, "Listen, I've been hearing about these things, and I've never received an invitation. I've never been to a pot party, and yet I get invitations to dinner and invitations to fraternities and sororities. How come?" They said, "No, No, No." I thought, "Oh my God, I'm being rejected." And they said, "No, you don't need to be turned on. You turn yourself on. You turn us on. You don't need pot." I realized they were paying me a tremendous compliment. What they were seeing there was a kind of energy. And out of this energy I find my work.

Can you add something more about what you've liked about university life and teaching?

Besides the relationship I had with faculty in other departments and the expectations I had for my students, I also had a very good relationship with members of my own department. It was nice. In other words, we had our own kind of art center here—our own New York, as I'm sure is happening on all campuses.

I suddenly realized that these people were just human beings like everybody else; they have their own inhibitions, frustrations, and some of them want to succeed so very, very badly that they'll make any sacrifice except the ultimate one, which is to turn their backs on teaching and invade the market wherever it may be, whether it's New York, or Germany, or London. I find artists truly middle-class, in that sense.

They are the least contentious members of this community, I find. They do not become involved in any revolutionary movements.

So in a sense I'm disillusioned with the artists and slightly disillusioned with the students. I'm disillusioned with the other members of the faculty. I'm disillusioned with the university. The most tragic thing is that I'm disillusioned with myself.

There is one thing that intrigues me about teaching: if I have twenty-five students, I want twenty-five different points of view, and I lose the point if I get two or three that are similar in any way. And yet I can't impress the students with the fact that they are unique, distinct individuals, you know, and that they are something special. They strive so desperately to be ordinary, to be just like everyone else, and I just can't understand it. And this is what my colleagues do.

They're in a kind of a dilemma. I found this out two years ago on my sabbatical in Europe. From Stockholm to Athens, wherever I went, the same thing was happening. I think that the faculty have become members of the establishment, and it is the thing that I find most disheartening. I recognize the fact that I too am a member of this establishment.

But the type of ambition I see is so fruitless, so hopeless, and I just don't see how it's going to help the world because it's so self-serving. And this is basically my disappointment with the faculty, with the university. At one point I felt that all the answers were there because that's where all the brains were. This is where all the asses are—they're not brains! They're not concerned with the world; they're only concerned with themselves—their own sacrosanct little area.

I don't know where else to turn for hope. Certainly not the church anymore. Not politics. In some ways I still think it may be with youth.

I've known you for perhaps fifteen minutes, but you seem a very intense person. At least you speak with great feeling and intensity about what you believe. Maybe it's asinine of me to say it, but I don't know whether you can expect everyone else to function at your level of intensity all the time. You may be expecting too much of people.

Well, what am I supposed to do: function at their levels of apathy? Some of my colleagues are minding the store constantly, you know; by this I mean they're in their studio and they're burning the midnight oil and they're neglecting their lovely wives, their beautiful children, and food, and drink, and conversation. They're putting out these grubby paintings that nobody gives a good goddamn for. These paintings are meaningless, absolutely meaningless. Painting is meaningless because it hasn't changed our American civilization as I can see it. It hasn't changed our way of life one iota.

And it's important to you that it change?
Oh yes.

Then why are you a painter?
I paint for my own amazement and amusement, *but* I paint as a last resort.

After what?
I'd rather enjoy a drink or two, preferably with a lovely female, or someone I can talk to without deluding him in any way or being aware of the fact that he may judge me or prejudge me. He'll automatically say, "Well now, relax. Blow your top!"—just as I may be doing now—without leaving and saying, "Gee, is he sick," or "My God, he's dangerous," or something like that.

I can only feel alive if I can relate to someone else. I find this very important.

But I cannot relate, in terms like I used to, to my own painting, because I was painting for something else. In my younger days I was painting for a career. Well, that goddamn career—I think that it's the biggest insult to me to discover that I've devoted a whole life to painting, and the only satisfaction I've gotten out of it is from a peripheral area which is teaching. I find this very sad.

But am I supposed to be brought to my knees? We're not building cathedrals anymore. We're building medieval monuments by certain architects for their own fame and glory, but they're impassive and they're massive, and they have nothing to do with man himself. I think they're edifices to these architects themselves. In a way I think that's what we've been doing: I think the easel painter or the sculptor has been doing the same thing. I think we've all deluded ourselves and I think this is very bad because somehow what has happened to humanity shouldn't have happened. No one speaks to anyone anymore. Everybody mistrusts everybody and there's no verbal movement, no flow, no give-and-take.

What are you so angry at yourself about?

The fact that my work has brought me something that most people in the university strive desperately to achieve. In other words, say a man will spend his entire life to become a professor, right? Getting tenure—these are the goodies that are offered to him. I have a notion that these are meaningless things in themselves. The thing I'm interested in is art and I find that there is no room for the type of art that I'm producing; not only for the type of art that I'm producing, but there's no room for the type of art that my colleagues are producing.

You know a funny thing: there is only room for the type of art that the wives of other professors are producing. There's only room for amateurism.

Have I caught you at a bad time? Are you down? Are you low today?

I don't know. I may be a little bit physically exhausted.

I ask because it seems to me that our conversation in thirty minutes has made a complete arc. You began talking by saying you were very enthusiastic, that you woke up in the morning delighted just to see what the new day would bring, you were so excited about your first day of class that you couldn't sleep last night, that you were always anxious to see what new contacts would bring. Then a little later, it began to sag. You were saying, "I'm disillusioned with the students, with the university, dissatisfied with my faculty colleagues." I think what I'm trying to tell you is that I don't understand where in the world we are.

Let me ask some more questions and maybe I'll get a clearer idea. What do you think has happened to your own work? You've tried to give me the impression that your own work isn't very important to you, but I don't believe that.

There are certain things that are inevitable, in my opinion. I think that the productivity of any individual (and I don't care what the hell he's producing or manufacturing) will continue in one form or another, for better or worse. I've had my ups and downs. There's a certain energetic element that has been missing in my work for a while. I know that in 1961 or '62 I had my most meaningful and most important show in New York. It was very important from a critical point of view (our lives are, so to speak, ruled by these people). It was also somewhat successful commercially. I mean I really felt like "I'm on the threshold of something," and this was only twelve years ago. I had worked hard for it and I had gotten to this point, and I really felt that there was a rhyme and reason for my life and to my work. Then of course I got involved in something else.

Well, all my energies went into it. I suddenly realized that you just can't teach out of your back pocket, you know, with your left hand. Sometimes when I come home I'm exhausted. I can be exhausted when I spend a day at the university. It's not just the classroom. I want my students to come and see me and I want them to come and see me not for their sake so much as for my sake, because I know that somehow or other they will clue me as to where I'm letting them down as a teacher, and what kind of information they want and how to reach them. Somehow I have egotistical faith in myself that I am a good teacher because I think of myself as a missionary, I think of myself as a priest, being a teacher, and I think of myself as a guru, a philosopher, and I think of myself as an unusual person. I think very well of myself in many respects.

It sounds to me as though you really take teaching very seriously.
I think this is the most influential aspect of anyone's life. I don't mean just the teaching; I mean the receiving. In my own way, the most influential people in my life were my teachers.

If the students see I'm in my office, they automatically drop in no matter what I'm doing. If I'm doing correspondence, or if I'm painting, or doing something else, I will stop whatever I'm doing and visit with them because I feel that they have priority over any activity that I'm doing. That's what this factory is designed for: it's for them, it's not for me. It's not for the administration, it's not for the bureaucracy; it's for the student, and the point is that too many people forget this. That university, that factory, is designed primarily for the student.

And that's going to cost you a lot so you're not going to be doing as much creative work of your own, but apparently you don't care so much about that at this point in your life.
I'll tell you one thing: I'm doing better work today than I have ever done in my entire life. And I do it with less hassle. I can go there when I'm feeling right, and I can do more in one hour today than I could in a week previously. And the work that I did in a week would be unnerving to my entire family.

Are you more interested in Walter Kamys, artist, or in Walter Kamys, human being?
Kamys, human being.

Are you more interested in Walter Kamys, teacher, or Walter Kamys, artist?

I'll be very honest with you. I'm being paid as Walter Kamys, teacher. This is where my income, livelihood, where my responsibility is.

If you're so alienated now, are you thinking about pulling out of the university?

If I had an alternative, yes. But I'm a coward. I've reached a point in my life where I'm trapped, in a sense. I'd like to pull out, but where the hell would I go? What would I do? There's no escape.

Here's what I'd like to do: find, say, ten, fifteen, twenty acres in Maine, isolated, with some kind of a view, and I'd then join every book club in the world and every record club in the world and I'd have visitors coming in every weekend. This is my idea of the good life.

Art is simply without meaning in the United States. The only time you read anything about art today is at auction times. Every time a Rembrandt brings in several million dollars, this is important news. It's an economic thing. I remember a survey made by some economist: if you had bought stock like A.T.&T. at whatever it was selling for, and you also bought Cézanne, the A.T.&T. stock at that particular point couldn't touch the value of a Cézanne or a Renoir. And this is the yardstick that the Americans use.

I don't feel deprived financially. I don't think I have any bitterness there. I'm well paid for what I'm doing. I'm content and it certainly supplies my needs. But somehow, I still have a feeling that there's a spot in me that hasn't been fulfilled. And the university hasn't fulfilled it for me, and maybe I'm angry at the university for that. And what is it? I don't know. I really don't know. I'm not in love, for instance. I'm not in love with whatever it is that one must be in love with to be highly productive and energetic. Life isn't that meaningful for me—as it was in the past. I'm sure it can be, it will be. I'm looking for it. I haven't given up in any way.

I already said I only paint when I absolutely have to; when

I'm going out of my goddamn mind, I may go home and paint for a while. Somehow it refurbishes me, replenishes some juices I need. But I know this much: I could never again put in seven days a week, eight or ten hours a day as I used to. That would be absolutely without meaning.

John McCollum

John McCollum was born in Coalinga, California, February 21, 1922. He studied at the University of California at Berkeley (B.A.).

Mr. McCollum maintains an active concert, oratorio, and opera career, appearing regularly with leading symphonic and choral associations and in recitals throughout North America. He has recorded for Columbia, Decca, RCA, Westminster, Desto, and Word.

Mr. McCollum teaches at the University of Michigan and is director of the University Division of the National Music Camp at Interlochen.

Mr. McCollum, how was it you decided to become a professor in a university?

I had expected that I would be associated with a university someday. I say "university" rather than "conservatory" because I did not particularly like the idea of living in a big city. Even in New York, where we lived for about fifteen years, we did not live in the city. So the idea of a university community environment appealed to me. I joined a university faculty probably five to ten years earlier than expected. The reason was that there was a rather sudden opening at Michigan. The school of music wanted a tenor with professional performance experience. That summer I was in Santa Fe with the opera company. I was invited to interview for the position. That was in late June, 1962.

I was involved in three operas and had a big slate of engagements for the next season, so it was a heavy decision to make because I was a very busy singer. But I flew to Ann Arbor and was offered the position. I hadn't even been thinking about this except as a projection for the future.

Well, as you are aware, there are a lot of economic insecurities in a professional singer's life. I was terribly busy, but if one has a health problem and has to cancel (I once had to cancel everything for five months), that means no income. If one has a family facing college (which I did; we have two children), one makes decisions based on economic security. Of course I knew that I could continue with my New York management, Columbia Artists.

I really enjoy the cultural advantages of a university center like this. There are so many things here in the arts. And I love sports: I love going to the games. So those advantages have a great appeal for me.

Had you taught at all while you were living in New York?

No, I had not taught except in totally different fields. The only teaching experience I had concerned flying. For two years I taught ground-school aerology, navigation, and aerodynamics. (In the navy I was a flight instructor in fighter-type aircraft for one year.)

What kind of feelings did you have about teaching voice, then?

Well, I thought I would try it for a while. I agreed to come here for a year. I did not move my family. We had a home near New York and I had a great number of engagements there that year, so I was, in effect, commuting. Also, it gave me a chance to settle down as a teacher. After two semesters, I decided that I liked teaching so we decided to move here.

What's so satisfying about teaching?

If you have a student with vocal talent and you help develop that talent plus all the elements of musicality (whatever they are) and help bring them together in a refined, well-coordinated way, the result is highly rewarding. Musicianship is an absolutely fundamental consideration. Naturally, the development of voice technique is also of primary importance, but those two must come together in one.

How does that satisfy, or change, or somehow reward John Mc-Collum?

It is very gratifying. Any teacher is a beneficiary of the forces of fate when a really talented student comes into his studio. If there is anything a teacher needs, it's a good student. My old teacher used to say, "The student makes the teacher," not the other way around. When we're dealing with such a demanding thing as art, we're looking for extraordinary talent. Raw potential which fails to develop is simply frustrating.

You know, one can "buy" a performance which is idiosyncratic *if* it's done artistically and with conviction and taste, and so what if there is a little rubato which you aren't really sure is right, etc., if it comes off beautifully and effectively. You can take it because there's something individual about it. That's what interests me most. I like to help students find their own interpretation of a song. Naturally I try to steer them on what I personally might think is the right course, but to have them come through with something good which seems to be really theirs—that is the most gratifying thing of all.

Basically, I would say the biggest weakness in college voice teaching is that the students are too young, but we're dealing with the institution of education in the United States. If a student is interested in a bachelor's or master's degree, this is going to take him about six years, from the age of eighteen to twenty-four. If you don't allow people into your program at the age of eighteen, you're not going to get any students. So we're stuck with that. I myself never had a voice lesson until I was twenty-four. I find that a lot of students have problems simply because they're not physically developed yet. It has nothing to do with emotional or intellectual maturity; it's physical development which they lack. I think we push them too fast to try to get them through a degree program, and we expect development from them which many are simply incapable of achieving. You know, a singer's best years are between the ages of thirty and fifty—with some obvious exceptions, of course.

What do you think has been the effect on your own performance career of these twelve years at Michigan?

I've benefited. I taught flying at a time in my life when I had not had a lot of training. When I started to teach flying, then I realized I didn't know much about flying. I had to think about this a great deal. It helped me as a pilot. Well, I think in singing there's no question that as you try to seek answers for students you begin to see things in a much more detailed way. Up to that point, I had known only my own experience. One learns a great deal from experience but one doesn't learn *everything* from experience. In trying to relate what I'd learned to students, I began to think about it from different angles.

Every student is unique. His background is different from every other student and it is reflected in how he sings. Sometimes what works with one student simply doesn't work with another; so you remain flexible in how you relate ideas. Basically we're dealing with only a few fundamental things. We're dealing with breath—how you get it and how you spend it; we're dealing with the vocal mechanism—the larynx; we're dealing with pitch; we're dealing with language; and we're dealing with resonance (I put resonance last because it's affected by language: whether a vowel is large or small; whether it's nasalized.) Those are the five elements of singing. But each student's physical makeup is different. Some are very quick and others not, so we're dealing with a number of variables.

I don't consider myself a "vocal mechanic"—that there is an a, b, c, and that's it and one must do it this way. I don't believe in rigid "musts." The only "must" I believe in is that one must achieve an effective performance. That's the goal. I relate a great deal to sports. My old teacher used to say, "Form in sports is technique in singing." You may see eighteen different stances for eighteen different players at bat, yet they all can hit the ball. Some are better than others, but they wouldn't be in the major leagues if they couldn't hit. Just so, you don't take a singer and try to make him fit into a mold. You could destroy something basically good and unique. Somebody said, "If you have a good student, the most important thing is to *not* get in his way." I believe that too. The idea is not to block the student. So it's a very individual thing and it can't help but be interesting if you look at it that way.

Are you a better singer now for having taught?

Yes, I believe I am in many ways. The reason is those five fundamental things I mentioned before have become more important to me. I've seen tension building in a student in the same way I've experienced it myself. The fundamental thing, the smart thing, is to be able to release tension. I've developed an attitude in my own singing to prevent the building of tension. I won't say it's foolproof (I don't think anything is foolproof), but it has helped me. Voice technique is a collection of habits. Hopefully they're good, productive habits. One of the habits I've found constructive in my own work, particularly since I've been teaching, is the habit of releasing tension from the area of my throat, my tongue, my jaw, the trunk of my body, or my whole body, on the intake of every breath. Every breath should be refreshing. Every breath should trigger a release of any tension which may have occurred during the last phrase. It's a constructive thing. Just that one thing (and there are many others) has been more deeply ingrained in me since I've been a teacher, because I've found it necessary to stress it over and over again with students.

I think my attention to the detail of languages, good diction, nuance have improved. One hears mistakes from students with frequency and one begins to see where the real problems are because so many make similar mistakes. On the other hand, some have quick, good ears, you start to see little mistakes with them which previously hadn't seemed very serious to you. You begin to view it in more detail and it sharpens your ability to enunciate words properly.

We've been talking about positive things. I'm also interested in negative things. How has university teaching frustrated you or stood in your way as an artist?

It hasn't stood in my way. I'd have to say that being away from New York and my management has been a disadvantage: I've simply had less and less contact with them. It's a disadvantage not to be on the New York scene. There are thousands of performances there, and I used to participate in a good many of those. Being here has cut me off because I'm not readily available to do this or that on short notice. This has naturally cut down my circle of acquaintances on the big scene. The personnel in the scene change. There are many new conductors and singers whose names I've only seen in the *New York Times*. I don't know them personally. I used to be right there. That's true of management as well. That's been a disadvantage as far as staying active in the profession is concerned.

However, from an age standpoint, one expects to wind down anyway, particularly if he is a singer. A singer is similar to any athlete. After a certain age, he is less able to do certain things. Sometimes he gets better at certain things. I think I am better today in some ways. But I know, on the other hand, it isn't as easy for me to sing Bach as it used to be. You know, the tessitura is such that at my age it just isn't as easy for me to sing it anymore.

At some stage of the game, one feels that he hasn't accomplished anything. I don't care who you are or where you are. You feel, "Gee, I haven't really done anything. It wouldn't have meant a blasted damn to the world of music if I had just stayed on that little old newspaper." That's probably true. It didn't make a bit of difference, not a ripple on the surface of the whole body of music. You feel that way and it's frustrating and depressing. But recently I got up a resumé, and I realized, "My God, I really have done a lot. I've been a lot of places." I've sung with at least a hundred orchestras and as many conductors. I never sang with Toscanini, I'm sorry to say, and I never sang with George Szell, but with practically everybody else. I've sung over forty leading opera roles, and much, much oratorio—practically everything. So if I look at lists of things, it looks like quite a bit.

There is one thing which I find annoying in university life. I wouldn't be honest with you if I didn't mention this. I'm basically a democrat. I believe in freedom. Although I understand the pacifist's point of view, when the chips are down I'll fight if my freedom is threatened. But I think *over*-democratization has developed in universities. It's become almost hilariously silly. It's become a maze of red tape and committees studying committees studying committees. You can't make any kind of decision without going through three, four, or five stages of committee structure. I think as a result, freedom has been democraticized right out of our activity.

It's come to the point where no matter how much you've done, no matter how much you think you've won your spurs, no matter where you've been or under what circumstances you've performed, your opinion is no more worthwhile than anyone else's. I don't think everyone knows everything. Surely, if I want another faculty member's advice, I'll ask for it—assuming he knows more about the matter than I.

There has to be direction. You can't drift around in decision-making. You need someone at the helm. It's terribly important. Someone has to say, "Yes, this can be done; no, that cannot be done," and let it go at that. That's why you have people appointed in directorial jobs. In a committee you have five or six points of view and what you come out with is a great big omelet instead of a soufflé.

You might say, "Well, I thought you were in favor of freedom!" I *am* in favor of freedom—regulated so that we can live together; that's what democracy is for. But sometime, someone must be empowered to make a decision without having to assemble five committees. For me, that's become increasingly hard to live with. University faculties have voted themselves into a morass of *non*-decision-making.

Mr. McCollum, since coming here you've done a lot to attract to this voice department exactly the kind of artist-teacher I'm very interested in.

If I can take any credit for that at all (and I'm not sure I can), I'll say it's because I believe in it. If you want a professional school, then by heaven get professionals. I believe "on-the-boards" experience is the most important of all.

Robert Palmer

Robert Palmer was born June 2, 1915, in Syracuse, New York. He studied with Howard Hanson and Bernard Rogers at the Eastman School of Music, and later with Aaron Copland and Roy Harris. He received an Award of Recognition from the National Institute of Arts and Letters, two Guggenheim fellowships, and a senior Fulbright research grant.

Among a fairly large catalog of works, he is best known for his sonatas and chamber works, which have been performed widely, published, and recorded.

Mr. Palmer teaches at Cornell University.

Mr. Palmer, what were the factors involved in your decision to enter the academic community?

Well, very briefly, I entered the Eastman School of Music in 1931 with an idea that I would be a pianist although I had had a great deal of interest in composition. I actually had not thought very much about an eventual career but I suppose I had an idea that I would teach in a university.

I eventually majored in composition and studied with Hanson and Rogers and minored in piano. So at that point it seemed that I would be headed for university teaching.

I think it was quite apparent even at that time (especially at that time, I should say, but I don't think it has actually changed that much) that a living was simply not possible outside of university circles. I was not of a temperament to go and try my luck in New York and try to make my reputation purely from the composition standpoint.

As a result of your affiliation with a university, what have been your major satisfactions and what things have frustrated you in your dual role as a university professor and composer?

I'll speak quite frankly now because I have been giving this a great deal of thought. I think that I have found the university environment temperamentally suited to my particular nature, which is in some measure reflective and in some measure perhaps even philosophically oriented. I have developed a great commitment to teaching. I love teaching. I find it extremely rewarding to work with students and I find that my own growth and explorations of music have been enormously aided by this. On the other hand, I was pulled up short a number of years ago by a remark that Copland made in an article published in 1947. I was still relatively young in my career and there was an article which was later published in a book on music by Copland in which he said, "Palmer gives out too much of his energy at Cornell in his teaching capacity" (or words to this effect) and I more or less tossed that off in the early years. But more and more I recognize that this very commitment to teaching (considering the fact that I have carried a particularly heavy load, being chairman of graduate committees and in general administering the composition and theory programs as well as a quite full teaching load) has in fact sapped energy that I perhaps could have spent in further composition.

Originally my teaching involved a great deal of beginning or more elementary theory courses, and as my career developed I began to move to the upper division undergraduate, and eventually largely to graduate courses. In recent years I just haven't had the opportunity to teach undergraduates. My attitude about this is changing at this point. I think that the undergraduates present here fifteen or twenty years ago were an entirely different sort than the more recent student. The more recent student is I think brighter on the whole, less rigid, has a more exploratory nature, and on the whole is a much more stimulating kind of student to deal with. Whereas perhaps my major thrust of interest in years past was to move more into the graduate area, I find more recently a regret that I am not having more contact with undergraduates because they seem to be a different breed.

I actually have enjoyed working with students of varying abilities and varying temperaments and I seem to have been able to do this with some reasonable amount of success—not completely, of course. It isn't that I only find satisfaction working with a certain kind of student. Of course there is satisfaction working with a student who is sensitive and productive. Anyone would feel and say that, but this is by no means the kind of thing I am limited to.

You touched briefly, a few moments ago, on your own work. Could you enlarge a little bit on that? What has happened to your own artistic output as a result of being affiliated with the university?

Well, I think that is a little hard to say except in extremely general terms. I suppose that as far as output is concerned, I have continued to compose an average of one large-scale work a year. In many cases, the bulk of the composition occurs during the summer. If a commission has been in the offing, I have been able to make time during the year to work. Of course it's much more difficult when your course commitments and individual student commitments are relatively heavy. When you are involved in completing a work of any large scale, you need a fair amount of concentration on that and I think that the various teaching and other commitments do tend to interfere. For instance, this past year I worked rather hard for three or four months not making very much headway. Partly it was simply bad luck, but also partly that I just couldn't concentrate. By contrast, I have been relatively free, and I have written perhaps half again as much in three weeks as I wrote in three months during the regular term. I must say that this previous experience of bad luck is rather unusual, but it does seem to be happening a little more often than it used to. Some composers have said that writing music becomes more difficult as you get older rather than less so.

Correct me if I am wrong, but I get the feeling from your remarks that this isn't a big problem for you.

No, I have never felt that. In fact, I was asked at one point to contribute a piece to the College Music Society on a remark that Stravinsky had made to the effect that the university was not the place for the serious composer. I was not able to make that contribution because of various circumstances, but if I had made it, I would have certainly said that I didn't feel that. One person who did contribute said that he felt the university or any other circumstance had advantages and disadvantages and that composers simply make the best of whatever situation they are in. As far as our society is concerned, I think that the university (unless you have some kind of complete subsidy and complete freedom either through independent finances or some kind of government grant which is almost nonexistent) is about as good a situation as one could hope for. It's actually more than this for me: I feel at home in the university and I thrive on the intellectual stimulation. I am extremely interested in ideas in general and find all of this and the contact with students and with the music that I must explore in dealing with students to be a source of growth for me.

I teach a number of courses in musical analysis and I think there is a notion abroad that if you analyze a piece of music, you somehow kill it. Well, there is perhaps some grain of truth in that. I suppose that a piece that I have analyzed extremely thoroughly note by note is never quite the same. At the same time, there is so much revealed about the piece and about the mastery of the composer that cannot be gotten any other way, that it seems to me the rewards of that kind of thing vastly outweigh the other.

I think that there are some temperaments, there are some kinds of artists, who perhaps would not thrive in a university. If you are the kind of individual whose temperament is suited to the reflective and contemplative aspects of life and to whom ideas are stimulating, and where the contact with students is a rewarding activity, then I think it's all right. You have to remember that most of the great composers, in addition to performing, were teachers. They taught privately to be sure, and of course not in an institution, but basically made a good deal of their living by teaching. That's often forgotten.

How are your relations with colleagues here?

This department has been extremely fortunate; in fact it has some reputation, I think, for the fact that people who have come here have been picked primarily on the basis of professional excellence in some particular area. At the time they were chosen, it was hoped they would fit in (from the standpoint of interests and temperament and so forth) with the department as it existed. The department has been amazingly lucky in this respect so that it exists in a state of considerable mutual respect and has operated for many years more like a family than like a professional department. I hear that in other areas things are not necessarily all that harmonious, but I think that the department is relatively free from the kind of professional jealousy that does seem to plague some places. Therefore my relationships with my colleagues have been rewarding and productive on the whole.

They are not jealous of you?

Well if they are, there is very little evidence of it. Quite, quite the contrary.

Let me ask you another kind of question. If I had a school somewhere and I wanted to attract you to it, aside from salary (which we all understand and appreciate) what would I have to offer you? What kind of school would it be ideally? What kind of things would go on there?

I think the sort of place that could attract me would have three or four ingredients. For one thing, I think I probably would be interested in a composer-in-residency status in the sense that a certain part of my load would be recognized as simply the performing of the basic function of composing, which is what I am best constituted to do. At the same time, I would not like to be divorced from teaching because I would like an opportunity to work with students, but perhaps on a freer basis. I would like, for instance, in dealing with older music perhaps, to circumvent the usual course offerings and teach an exploratory course where if I wanted to deal with sixteenth-century music one day and Domenico Scarlatti the next and Paul Hindemith the third, I would have the freedom to do this. That is, to explore, let's say, a certain aspect of music regardless of a particular period, so that I'm not teaching eighteenth-century counterpoint or sixteenth-century counterpoint or something like this.

I also enjoy those courses and would from time to time perhaps want to teach them, but I would like to try working with composers both from a creative side and also from the course side more on an apprentice basis, with somewhat greater freedom than the present setup of course offerings affords.

Another thing certainly would be to have sufficient performing resources so that the students could immediately hear the kinds of things they are doing, even in the course of writing a piece, even though the piece isn't completely finished— perhaps only a passage could be copied out and performed so the student could see what mistakes he was making. These same musicians would also be there, of course, to perform works by the faculty.

Another thing I would like to see (and this would be for the university in general) would be an educational series on twentieth-century music in which standard and even more recent twentieth-century works would be done in open rehearsal and then presented in concert, where the musicians or members of the faculty would talk about these works to students with relatively little background, to build up an audience on the campus. I think the university is missing a tremendous bet here and I think this thing would be something you could involve the composers themselves in as a teaching resource and it would be a tremendously valuable thing to be going on on the campus. As far as I know, it's happening very, very seldom, if anywhere.

I am extremely interested in the relationships between twentieth-century art and the directions in which the world is moving and some of the intellectual and even theological currents. I think that musicians tend on the whole to stay too much within their own discipline. Of course it's extremely demanding, but I think that musicians ought to have an opportunity to realize their art in a larger context. I would like to be part of some inter- disciplinary institute at which things like this could be ex- plored. Those are some of the things that would go on in a place I might be attracted to.

Rudy Pozzatti

Rudy Pozzatti was born January 14, 1925, in Telluride, Colorado. He studied at the University of Colorado (B.F.A., M.F.A.) and with Wendell H. Black, Max Beckmann, and Ben Shahn.

His paintings and prints are held in collections of the Museum of Modern Art, the Library of Congress, the Art Institute of Chicago, and elsewhere. His work has been shown in numerous exhibitions both in the United States and abroad. In 1969 the University of Nebraska assembled a twenty-year retrospective of his work.

He is Distinguished Professor at Indiana University.

Had you originally set out to be a teacher?
Not at all.

Why did you start to teach, then?
Well, the two people whom I credit for a great deal of influence in my early life are Max Beckmann and Ben Shahn; both of them, of course, are world-renowned artists; both, unfortunately, are dead now. My prime concern has always been to be an artist. The creative aspect has been the strongest thing in my life all these years.

I didn't really know what I was going to do, to be honest with you. When graduation came, I sort of asked myself, "Now what the hell am I going to do?" Suddenly this job came up and I said, "Oh, what the hell, for a year I guess I can teach."

At least it was some kind of security.
Yes. Of course you know the pay in 1950: I got $3,000 for my starting pay. But at least it was a beginning; I knew they had a good workshop and I could continue my work, and that was the important thing.

Then what happened to you?
Ben Shahn and I had been corresponding and he interested

me in applying for a Fulbright. Since my mother and father were both born and raised in Italy, he thought it was important for me to get back to see the country of my parents and find my real roots. So I applied and fortunately I got a Fulbright grant. So in the fall of 1952, my wife and I went to Italy for a year.

Then I came back, taught for two more years at Nebraska, and then I moved from Lincoln and came here to Indiana University.

You've been here since 1956?

On the records, I've been here since fall semester, 1956, but I've been away a great deal of the time. I think the fact that I've been able to get out of here many times since 1956 (which breaks up the period of work and time very nicely) has been important.

Let's talk a little more generally for a few minutes, and then maybe I could ask some more pointed questions if you don't mind. What since 1956 have been your principal satisfactions and rewards and what have been unhappy times, unhappy things involved with being a university professor?

Well, I have to admit that for all of us who are interested in creative pursuits in a specialized area (this would be people interested in sculpture, ceramics, printmaking, weaving, perhaps), all the creative areas where there is a great deal of equipment and space involved, none of us at the end of our graduate time would have enough money to afford any of these things. It takes years to accumulate adequate facilities and equipment. I think it's good that you can go into a situation where you are teaching but also have the use of all this equipment. I think also the students are very fortunate in the same respect.

You can set aside specific time in your schedule in order to put time into the workshop. Those are positive things. I was fortunate here at Indiana to come into a relatively young department (with a lot of people my own age) and a tremendous kind of initiative and drive among all the young people, and this still continues. I don't mean to say that we're all killing each other

competitively, but I think that the interest another person
brings to you is very important. Not only have I found that here
but in other places where I've gone. The kind of person you
meet at a university adds to that.

I must say also that the better students do the very same
thing. The advanced students and certainly a great number of
the graduate students in many of their crazy, kooky ways (and I
don't mean this in the sense of their dress, or habits, or attitude
because I admire much of that) have crazy ideas of what they'd
like to do. Part of that is almost impossible, but a lot of it is at-
tainable. And I think if a person is receptive and open he can
see possibilities of his own work advancing through the ideas
of the students. I think that's very important. And as most graduate schools bring students from all areas of the country, in a
sense you have a kind of seismographic recording of the
thoughts and feelings of many places around the United States
at one time in your own locale. I think this is important.

You're from Ann Arbor; you have a great university there. I
find the same thing here at Indiana. With many of my friends in
the music school and other disciplines, I find a great deal of
exchange. We have a fine music school, opera, all of the things
which I like very much. We're culturally isolated without the
university. Bloomington is a town of 45,000 people. There
would be no museum, no symphony, no ballet, no chamber
music. You know, you'd really be hard up for the kinds of
things that I like to hear and see. The university has certainly
provided this. Guest speakers who come in from all over the
United States—even abroad; visiting students and faculty from
abroad; the Artists' Series: I think you could go on forever. You
have to also realize you can't possibly take all of this in, but at
the period of time where you think you want it, it's there for
you.

Do you like to teach?

Yes, if all I had to do was teach, that is, to meet the students
in the workshop. My teaching is different: I don't have to pre-

pare a forty-five-minute lecture and get in there and do my thing and entertain students or try to edify them in a certain way. My job is to bring out what I consider to be some of the individualistic qualities of each student. I find a great deal of satisfaction doing that in the atmosphere that I love very much—a print workshop.

Are there times when you don't like to teach?

Yes, to be very honest. There are times when maybe I'm very engrossed in my own work, if I've gotten a commission or if I'm working on something of more than everyday importance. Maybe I've gotten a thread of something going and I find I have to drop everything and go to the class, and I often find, coming back to the work, I've lost that initial spark or the thing that would have really brought something out—then the drudgery again of working yourself up to it. Sometimes I think you have to admit that in the creative pursuit it's that *moment;* it's fleeting and it's gone, and maybe what you start again will never take you in the same direction that one spark would have taken you.

Are there some students you don't like to teach?

Yes, although I have not found a great number of students (I think the percentage has been very small) that are really unreceptive in most ways. I think I have a world of patience, and my nature is one of relative calmness and a willingness to wait and to wait and to work. I have found with this small percentage of students that they are absolutely unwilling, unreceptive, and maybe they don't even belong in a university; they might have a future in some other direction that has no relationship to the university. Maybe it's certain aspects of the university that turn them off completely: the rigors of going to class and meeting a schedule, and all of that.

I'm not sure I understand precisely what you mean by "unreceptive" students.

That's a difficult thing to explain. No matter how I try to reach them, to find out what their interests are, what they would really like to do, no matter what I show them, what I suggest, just nothing happens. Whether their backgrounds haven't allowed them to reach a certain level of performance where they would be ready to do this, I don't have any idea.

But you're not complaining about lack of technique, and you're not complaining about what could in a gross way be called lack of talent (whatever that is); that wasn't what you said. You said "unreceptive."

Let's take it another way. Maybe I don't have a damn thing to offer them; therefore we don't really come together in any way. I think if a teacher is going to do his job, he has to give of himself to the student. The student has to find places within him where what you can offer can fit—not in the sense that you completely override the student's own creative pursuits. I've never done that to my knowledge, nor ever aspired to. But I think there is something that I can offer. Sometimes I think the greatest thing I feel I've done for some of the students is to really find what it is that they can say better than anyone else can say. I'm a strong believer in individuality, and one of the things I rebel against very much in all periods is the fact that everybody operates under the same wavelength. You know, we look at art today in a specific way. In order to really be "with it" you have to fall into that. I work hard against that.

If your job as a teacher is to somehow help bring to the surface whatever individual there is in that student, and then let him go his own way with whatever help he wants from you (or maybe doesn't want from you), what's so groovy about doing that for students?

Well, I think that this is really one of the things that students need more than anything else. You know we talk about "charisma." As an Italian, and as a Catholic, charisma means a special thing to me: it's the bringing of the Holy Ghost. I'm not an apostle; I don't go out and crusade; but this word means a great deal to me. I think that the way one lives and the way one works and the way one influences and affects students is very, very important. Sometimes maybe that is the most important thing I do for my students. My commitment to my work (which is not only exemplified in my own workshop when nobody sees me) is exemplified in the class workshop: the demands I make on the students, the use of the equipment, the tools, the demands I make on them as individuals—the responsibility they have as artists, as creative persons, to confirm their own ideas and beliefs in themselves and to have the strength and conviction when they go out to carry it forward. I think if I were not strong in my own convictions, they would not have very much when they left here either. So maybe the strength of my own work and convictions is the important thing when I walk into the workshop; maybe it isn't the pearls of wisdom one drops, but the kind of convicing attitude and manner of life that one has—I think maybe that's the thing.

I would want to think that for today's student this is pretty damn important—more than it has ever been in my short period of teaching. Young people today really look for the commitment in the man or woman.

If you were suddenly independently wealthy, would you continue to teach?

I've thought about that a lot, not in the sense that I hope someday somebody will drop a bundle in my lap; but I think it is important to constantly question why you're doing what you're doing. I'm forty-six, and you know, you say, "How long do I want to do this?" I have wondered if I got a lot of money suddenly if I would continue to teach.

The one thing I think I would be afraid of losing if I quit teaching is the association with other men and women in my field, the activity of the university or any place that's similar to it, and this strange quality that comes from the students. There's a lot of harassment from those people; you know, they make it tough for you at times. We've been through some pretty rough years. But despite that, I'm still afraid that removed from that atmosphere I would lose something.

Maybe you could ask me another question and say, "Don't you have enough faith in yourself, your own strength and convictions?" I do have that. But I think we all need some kind of agitation, disquieting influences, that rile you so that you don't run on a smooth road continuously. I think you've got to have it tough in order to really reach down inside your guts and find out if you really can hack it, whether this is what you can do better than anything else. The difficult times are pretty damn important.

You said some time ago that one of the exciting things to you here was the importance to you of active colleagues. Do you think that you could be persuaded to go to some small school as the only practicing artist on the faculty?

I wouldn't go. I like the elbowing. I was very active in sports, and I kind of like to get knocked around and do a little knocking myself—not in a malicious way, don't get me wrong. I don't like to dig anybody who's having difficulties creatively because we all have difficulty. But I'm kind of down on people who really have a responsibility to be creative; in other words, they are teaching or attempting to bring to younger people what it is that creativity is all about. If they're not involved in it, it's kind of a heresy; it just isn't right.

Now I think a person should be involved, struggling through all the problems—the medium itself, and the aesthetic problems. Then I think he has a legitimate right to be in that workshop talking to younger people about creativity.

Do you get along well with your colleagues?

I think so, by and large. I don't know of any of the people with whom I work at Indiana whom I have any ill feelings about at all. We have a big faculty. I've had differences of opinion with my colleagues which I think are important because we all represent different thrusts, different activities, and different feelings. I think the differences are just as important as the times when we can come together strongly.

Well, one of the differences is that you are unquestionably the most famous. You are certainly among your professional colleagues and peers the best-known artist on this faculty.

Listen, I think there are other people. We have other people who have not received as much notoriety who are still very good people.

I know that can happen. But do you ever feel any hint of jealousy because of your professional success among your colleagues?

No, I don't think so. The people with whom I've worked here have been exceedingly gracious about the good things that have happened to me. Just in my own defense, I have to say I don't do much blowing about it either. The papers may publish it, and so forth, but I've never used it even in my own job possibilities as a lever to say, "Don't you think I need a couple more thousand dollars' pay?" or "If you don't treat me right, I'm going to run over to the University of Michigan" or the like.

I've been proud of the accomplishment because it's taken a hell of a lot of work. I've got a very kind and loving wife and family who let me put in all the time. The faculty has not resented any of the good things. I would like to think that I've brought a little bit of help to them in a sense too, to know that the department is here and functioning and somebody is doing something.

You haven't said too much about what bothers you.

One of the things pretty high on my list is things that begin to encroach on the *time*. That time will not come out of your time with the students if you are committed to your job.

I find that committee work is really bugging the hell out of me; it's taking a lot of my time away from the studio and away from my thoughts about what I'd like to do at the university with the students.

I feel that committees exist because individuals in certain positions don't want to assume their responsibilities. Now that's a pretty strong statement, but damn it I feel in my own area that when I teach printmaking, if they want to condemn me for anything or praise me, it's because of the moves I've made and the initiative I've taken. I've been the director of that program, and it either lives or dies by what I do—but I take full responsibility for it. I would hope that if more people within a university structure were a little bit stronger there might be less work.

You have search committees looking for deans; you have search committees looking for chairmen; you have search committees looking for presidents of universities. I would say that when this man has been analyzed and dissected, and cut to pieces and re-put together—my God, if we haven't decided that he's the man for the job, then the whole thing is wrong.

He knows all the responsibilities of coming into a big university to take over a department or a series of departments as a dean or a president. Man, he's not blind when he comes in there. OK. If he comes in and says, "Yes, I want to do the job," and we have decided after fifteen of us have really looked at everything he owns—especially his wife and children (it gets pretty vicious at times on these committees, you know)—I would think that that man should then be trusted by the departmental members to do the job. Not to come, draw the pay, and then suddenly say, "Well look now, to do this we'd better form five committees."

Last year when I was gone they interviewed a man here. I got letters from everybody and they said, "Man, he's a tough son-of-a-bitch. He's gonna really knock some heads." I was delighted. I like to work for somebody like that; I think a professional recognizes another professional.

I hate to work for another kind of person who is just so amenable and so without conviction and direction that you're constantly fortifying that part of him instead of also doing your job. I think we need somebody in there (especially these days when money is tough) who just goes over there and says, "I've got to have that. If I don't get it, I'm going to steal it." I like positive people. If they're tough, and if they're after my ass to make me work more, that doesn't bug me—if they're *fair*. If they get malicious, then I don't dig that. But tough people who are professionally oriented and demanding I don't mind at all. I think that's what the world is all about.

What do you think has happened to your own creative output as a result of university affiliation?

I've had the chance to build this studio here at home, and in the last three and a half years I would say my output has almost tripled because of the studio. It increased a great deal when I came here and was given a studio in which to work. At Nebraska I didn't have a separate studio; I had to work in the shop where all the students worked. That was a real hassle.

I have a certain neatness and precision in the way I approach my work, and certainly in printing, everything has to be right and clean and proper. This is very difficult to do in a studio you're sharing with other people. So the facilities and the salary, and the prizes I've won because of the work I've produced, have allowed me to build this kind of shop and buy the equipment I need.

The affiliation with other faculty members involved in creative pursuits has been very rewarding. I've met a great number of visiting artists of high repute who have come here as lecturers and visitors. Just recently at commencement I had the honor of presenting Noguchi, the great Japanese-American sculptor, for an honorary degree. I spent three days with him which was really a delightful time. The trips: every time I have moved into another part of the world, I've always come back with sketchbooks full of stuff and ideas and it's always led to an avalanche of new work.

That has been really important. And then meeting people in other disciplines. One of my good friends in town is a pathologist; I've spent some time in his lab looking at slides and it's a magnificent world he's opened to me in those cell structures. I have good friends in mathematics and computing who are trying to get me interested in the use of computers for graphic arts. I don't know what that'll lead to, but I wouldn't have had those possibilities in other ways. A good friend of mine who just died recently was a stage designer here. He and I became very close because when he came here about nine years ago on a Fulbright from Italy he couldn't speak English. We got along beautifully. He opened up the world of stage designing to me.

Does the importance of these associations go for students as well?
Oh yes.

Do you believe in a so-called liberal education, general education?
Indiana University in the last two years has changed its curriculum for undergraduates in the college of arts and sciences (of which we are a part), and I think they've done the students a great service in opening things up for them and allowing them to do more things that I think are directly applicable to their own pursuits. The idea of a broad education (that you take a little of this and a little of that, etc.) if you're to go on and really fill in the gaps would be great. But I think people today are really more interested in getting to something; they don't like the irrelevance of a lot of things.

I think now they have the chance to do the things they want. Maybe what it does is put the whole responsibility on them instead of saying, "OK. You're a freshman now, and this is what you'll take, and as a sophomore, you'll take this." I want the student to make up his own mind. Our experiences may not necessarily take in all of his desires and his wishes. I think this is a period of trial and error. Let them find out what it is they really want to do. With grades and everything, it's very important to evaluate somehow or other, but we put too much stress on what that little grade is and not so much on what they might have gotten out of the thing. You know, you might have gotten a C and gotten a hell of a lot out of the course, so forget that it isn't a B or an A.

Ben Shahn and I were very close and I've kept this quote of his in a notebook. He believed that "It is the mission of art to remind man he is human." I use that a lot with my students and in my own thoughts and beliefs.

We kind of lose the whole idea of living, you know, what it is we're about. We get so damn involved in many things and we forget to replenish our souls just looking at a tree or at something someone made. I think it's important that we do it.

How could I get you away from this place? I'd like to know what kind of institution could steal you from Indiana University?

I would have to have facilities there. The salary is not everything; I really mean that. I don't want to have to go to some place and spend another three or four years building what I have. I would like to be again among people who would be demanding, inspiring, and motivating, and be within an area where I could have other cultural pursuits. I'd like to be able to visit museums, keep abreast of their exhibitions, symphonies, see an opera once in a while, meet different people.

So far, you've been telling me what you have here. Why would you move?

Well, I wouldn't.

What do you think are ways to elicit from first-class, producing professional artists some commitment to teaching in a university?

I think you should tell them that they do have a certain commitment. For lack of anything else, you have to talk about teaching schedules or loads. This would be a set number of hours per week with the students. "Handle that whichever way you wish, but you must find ways to meet and come together." If you could assure such a person that he wouldn't get embroiled in ninety other things, like committees, and give him a place to work, I think he'd be willing.

George Rochberg

George Rochberg was born July 5, 1918, in Paterson, New Jersey. He studied at the Curtis Institute and with George Szell, Rosario Scalero, and Gian-Carlo Menotti. He received Fulbright and Guggenheim fellowships and the George Gershwin Memorial Award.

Mr. Rochberg's works have been performed by major ensembles and soloists. His most recent compositions have received especially high critical and public acclaim.

Mr. Rochberg teaches at the University of Pennsylvania.

Mr. Rochberg, please tell me a little about your entry into academic life.

I spent a long time working as an editor and director of publications for a music publishing house. I was there from 1951 until 1960. In a curious way, I had all sorts of hankerings for academia. I began to get a little tired of the world of business and the business of editing and working on everybody else's manuscripts. This was an 8:30-to-5:00, everyday job, five days a week. I became a composer, I think, chiefly because I had a determined will. I did all of my writing at night, on weekends, and three glorious weeks of vacation every summer. So you can begin to get some sense of the internal pressure that was developing which drove me out of this kind of a life into teaching. People began to say to me, "You really should teach in a university." And I quite agreed with them. I thought I should too.

Why?

I was always rather articulate. That is, I always had the need to write down my thoughts. During these years I even published some theoretical pieces and some critical pieces—reflections on what was going on.

Parallel with that was also this very strong inner compulsion to begin to transmit these ideas from my own experience to students, and I began to feel that this curious combination of working in business and the little teaching I'd done at Curtis wasn't really entirely satisfactory. And there was, of course, also the necessity to continue to earn a livelihood.

If you came into a comfortable stipend, would you quit teaching right now?

I'd certainly give it very serious consideration for the simple reason that I'm past fifty. And even if we believe the actuarial tables of the insurance companies and assuming that my genetic structure is reasonably good, let's say I've got another twenty years. Well quite frankly, I'd much prefer to spend those twenty years putting down on paper what I feel and what I think in musical terms—much, much less now in prose—than to constantly be faced by the necessity of trying to work out a new topic or a new set of materials for a class of students.

We have problems of the varying quality of students. When I first began to teach at Penn, which was 1960, it was quite different. Psychologically, culturally, even politically, I think we were better off than we are now. And as I compare the students of that decade with students of this one, there's not only a vast difference, but the difference, I think, lies in degrees of maturity and degrees of seriousness. The kids I worked with in the 1960s were enormously serious. They were not all of equal gift or of equal intensity. But you have to remember, we're not just talking about a class of indifferent students who are coming to take a one-term course for credit. We're talking about kids who are very much like myself when I was a kid. They want to become composers, which means they've got all kinds of problems. They've got not only the problem of getting through their degree at the university, but they've got the problem of beginning to discover themselves as so-called creative artists.

I used to say to my students, "Don't be misled by the fact that we're sitting here between the ivy walls of the University of Pennsylvania. We're talking about art, we're talking about music, and we're talking about the standards of Bach and Beethoven and Brahms as far as I can understand them and can discuss them with you; we're talking about the necessity to develop powers of self-criticism, powers of taste, powers of discrimination, so that you know whether or not you're doing something good. This has nothing to do with course work or whether you get your degree or not. I'm not concerned with that. We're here for an entirely different purpose—one, in fact, which is, potentially at least, within the range of the university but not ordinarily thought of as being within the range of academic training."

Let me see whether I understand you exactly. You said you warned your students not to be misled. Was it some sort of detachment from the mainstream of intellectual and artistic life that you felt might be a problem? Courses can be games after all.

Yes, they can be games; they can also be destructive if you don't know what the reason for that particular course is, or that particular discussion is; if you don't have a long-range sense of what it is you're devoting yourself to. A young man comes to the university now and says, "I want to be a composer." Well, this is quite different from one who comes in and says, "I want to become an engineer," or an atomic scientist, or a mathematician, or what have you. I'm not in any way deprecating the creative capacities that human beings can bring to every other field. I happen to feel that all human beings essentially are creative. That is, we're all trying some way to find new insights and to discover truths about everything that we're involved with. But the reason for the point that I'm trying to make here with regard to young composition students in the university (and the reason why I can and do sometimes get quite excited about the whole thing) is that something about the atmosphere of an academic institution seems to rub away and gloss over the very hard, tough, and real problem of becoming a real artist. There is too much safety in taking a graduate degree. You're twenty-six years old, you get a job, go and teach in upper New York state or California or wherever, and you've now reached the lofty position of being an assistant professor, and if you have any brains in your head, the first thing you should ask yourself is, "How the hell am I going to become a composer? When do I take the necessary chunk of my life, in terms of time and energy, and devote it almost exclusively to searching out those things in myself out of which I'll make myself into a composer?"

And of course I feel that almost more than anything I can teach my students is just that attitude which I constantly make them look at. It may not always be the nicest way to do it, but sometimes you have to cut through certain kinds of curious complacent attitudes. Very recently, as a matter of fact, I said to a group of graduate students (most of whom were aspiring young composers), "Your average age is about twenty-three. Do you realize that Brahms, by the time he was nineteen, had written opus 5, the F Minor Piano Sonata; that Hector Berlioz by the time he was twenty-five or -six had written the *Symphonie Fantastique?* This is something for you fellows to think about. I'm not shortchanging the possibilities of what might happen to one of you—or hopefully, all of you. But there is something about the process of your education to which you lend yourselves which you've got to be on guard against, be very careful about. There's a certain kind of security and comfort in just coming to class every day or every other day, and after four or five years picking up your degree and then off and getting a job teaching. In the meantime, what's happening to the whole idea of becoming an artist?"

As a kid, somehow I knew that I was going to be a composer and that I had to find out how one put this stuff together. So it was then, that whole period in my teens, that I slowly began to make conscious for myself this awareness that to become an artist one had to be a craftsman—that there was no separation, really, between *what* you wanted to say and *how* you were going to say it.

I suppose my worst days as a teacher are when I come across precisely this kind of opacity; it's a kind of thickness or lack of a kind of inner spiritual spring—a hunger, a kind of appetite, you see. And so my experience as a teacher has been very intense, in that apparently I've been good for some people, very bad for others.

What you're saying is that these students have a somewhat naive or misguided notion of what they ought to be about. But you prefaced all this by saying you entered the university because you had a real desire to share with students some of your aesthetic notions. What's happened to your desire to do that?

I think probably a combination of things has happened. One is the fact of the erosion of time. Each year one is one year older. I have a very strong sense that I have a lot in me yet to say; I don't think I'm burned out by a long shot.

And a year gone is a loss. It's a little selfish, isn't it?

Very selfish; extraordinarily so. It's a little bit like "Give unto Ceasar that which is Ceasar's and unto God what is God's." I don't mean to sound presumptuous or pretentious or corny. But after having given to various kinds of publics a very large chunk of my life, I feel a very powerful need to devote myself almost exclusively now to my own work.

I've got three or four major projects—I mean really big works, any one of which will occupy me for at least a year or more. I'm happily thinking of them all simultaneously now. Obviously, I'll only do them one at a time. But the thought of going back to teach in the fall does not exactly turn me on.

I'm not putting teaching down because I don't want to stand up in front of a bunch of students. Sometimes I just simply lecture at them; I can't help it, I just am full up with something. I walk in and my feeling is, "I'm going to talk today and you're just going to listen." There are other times I walk in and I don't have anything to say, and they have to do the talking. If they're ready to talk and discuss things intelligently and with enthusiasm, we have a great day. If they're not, it's a bust—a complete, utter bust, let's face it.

I have a reputation of being tough. What I interpret this to mean is that I am demanding. Demanding of what? I don't give a damn about what kind of grades they get. But it comes down simply to the fact that I'm concerned about whether they have a developing sense of craft.

Help me understand something. You've said that you regard the coming fall's teaching with some reluctance. Is time the crucial variable more than anything else?

Yes, it's largely a function of time. I've just spent the month of May revising my First Symphony, which is a crazy thing to do—it's twenty or more years old—but I had to do it. I spent a good month. Now I've just finished this piano work. I've got a number of minor revisions to take care of on other works, things that are very important and are bothering me, and I don't want to delay them. Now I'm beginning to ask myself, "When am I going to copy out the new score of the First Symphony?" It's going to require it because I made very extensive, fundamental revisions. I've got to copy out the new piano work. I want to start the Fourth Symphony. I've got a large vocal work for which I just got clearance on the text, and I want to get going on that.

Now aside from any other projects that I'm thinking of, I see the months of June and July going. (Knowing my own rate of speed of work, I can pretty well calculate about how long it takes me to get something done.) I'm working up until the 15th of August, after which my wife, daughter, and I plan to take a trip just to visit some friends and relax.

We have an early calendar at Pennsylvania, so we begin right after Labor Day. Well, I've got two courses to prepare. Now this is not to say I haven't done any thinking about it: I've done a lot of thinking about it. As a matter of fact, I've already sketched out what I intend to cover in those courses and I've informed the students of one class, especially, what I will cover and what I think they ought to do to get ready.

Do you think you'd be any happier as a teacher if the only thing you did was guide these seminars for composers and not trouble yourself with any other kind of formally organized course?

Well, I used to think so. And as a matter of fact, most of my teaching was until recently just the seminar and private sessions—independent study. I know I'm beginning to contradict myself, but that's part of my whole nature and so it might as well emerge in this little session here. Whether I'm dubbed an avant-gardist or not (which I reject, incidentally, for all kinds of good reasons whatever other people may think), I am currently engaged in the struggle to become a tonal composer. Well, what I'm trying to say is, that to relearn (just like learning another language, or at least the subtle dialects of a language), I'm so concerned with these problems that I'm quite happy about the prospect of examining them with a bunch of students. So here I go contradicting myself.

So if in fact next year turns out to have been a good year as far as teaching goes, it will have been because I have this current obsession with the problem, and if the students are less hung up than they appear to have been the last couple of years, if they're more on their toes, and if they bring something more to the study than what some of them have been bringing the last couple of years, I think we'll make a real go of it. Then it will all have been worthwhile.

In a curious way, teaching a course is not unlike writing a piece of music. That is, if you've written a piece which you really like, then you never question the time, energy, effort; but if you've written a piece of music which turns out to be either bad (which is always possible) or unsatisfactory for all kinds of reasons (which is also always possible), you begin to question the instinct, the impulse, the effort and time, and so on. In other words, "Why did I do this? Why did I bother to do this?" There's always this kind of postmortem, self-critical, evaluative process after teaching.

Since teaching bears all kinds of responsibilities, I usually wind up every year with a feeling of intense dissatisfaction with myself, the feeling that I have not somehow conveyed, gotten across, not satisfied myself in terms of what it was I'd set out to do. Always this damnable verbal problem: the question of how can you find the words, the particular language, to convey what it is you're trying to say. You're trying to talk about art, you're trying to talk about the impulses that go into making art, you're trying to talk about the values of art; you're trying to talk about the difference between those things that separate a real piece of music from a piece which doesn't quite make it. This is all involved, and I've never quite had the feeling that I've really hit the nail on the head.

I've often asked myself, "What is my function as an artist in the university?" That is, what is an artist doing in an academic institution? Somehow, it seems to me that the university is the one institution which is available to us which can understand, not automatically, but can come to understand easily or more readily what our function is. At Pennsylvania, I'm happy to say, there's always been some not terribly well-formed but very profoundly instinctive grasp of what it was that I was trying to do.

It's interesting that at the same time I came to Pennsylvania, they brought others: writers, painters. This was a movement. So it wasn't as though I were alone. They were somehow supremely conscious of the importance of the simple presence of the guy who knocks his brains out trying to make a piece of art.

It sounds to me as though you ought to be very comfortable and rewarded by that atmosphere then.

If I've expressed any differences, fundamentally this is not to say that I feel I'm at odds with the university or that the university is at odds with me. I used to do a lot of proselytizing (which is really the right word). I always talked about opening a new wing—that it wasn't a question of altering the basic function of the university, that it wasn't a question of changing the purposes of the university, that it wasn't a case of contending with science or contending with other humanities. Essentially it was a case of establishing another wing. You've got this great house. Well, you've got some new members of the family.

You've got to provide them with a place to live and work, so open this new wing.

People seemed to understand this. I mean I didn't have to argue the case; that's the point I'm trying to make. They seemed to be ready to be convinced and persuaded. Now to be quite concrete about this, I needed to find some funds (and it was quite a chunk of cash, I must confess) to prepare the parts of my Third Symphony. After trying a number of things, including my own publisher, who didn't feel it was his obligation to support me in this way, as a last resort I thought of the university and went to the then-provost and explained my situation. After five minutes I came out with the assurance that I would have this money.

That little story tells a lot. It tells a lot about the university and about the artist within: that the university responded in five minutes, and that it was the last *place you went for help.*

Let me add this: what the provost said was, "We do this for other people—scientists—why shouldn't we do it for you?"

What are some ways, in your view, of attracting artist-teachers and retaining them?

To attract him you'd have to offer what he wants. What he wants is a place where he will be comfortable with his colleagues; a place where he at least has a minimum, a modicum agreement with their point of view; a place where the students are reasonably bright, active, talented. But more than anything else, I would suggest that what he wants is enough money on which to survive and enough time within which to work. In other words, the university should not make those kinds of demands which turn him into nothing but a hack.

What do you mean by "modicum of agreement with his colleagues"? What kind of colleagues does he want?

Well, obviously any place you're at you want to have some kind of easy communication about the things that interest you both. I can't imagine the artist-teacher, as you've called him, going to an institution doing a completely solo act.

You need your colleagues?
More than that I need the environment.

What is the environment?
Generally speaking, the situation in which there are colleagues with whom one can be sympathetic, where there's an atmosphere of making music, where there's that sense of seriousness. Certain kinds of schools are fine for the man with a mission who wants to go out and educate the masses. But I think there are appropriate actions for particular kinds of people, and a composer is hardly the guy that you would expect to have this kind of mission to accomplish.

And yet, in our hour and a half together, you've revealed yourself to me to be a very broad human being. Your intellectual life seems to be a very vivid thing to you. You have far-reaching interests.
Well, I'm behaving like the turtle now. I didn't years ago, but I'm doing it now out of necessity. I've got these works to do. The curious thing about writing music is the actual work of putting the thing down in terms of music. I literally need days when I don't see anybody except those closest to me (my family and possibly a few friends), when I have no distractions, when I'm really in my cocoon.

If I had to characterize myself psychologically, I tend to think of myself as someone who is obsessed, single-minded. I dislike any interference with my goals, I dislike any distractions which get in the way of achieving those goals. But nevertheless (and it seems contradictory), at the same time I've lived enough of a various kind of existence in the world to know that all of this is pointless and meaningless unless it happens "in the world."

Gyorgy Sandor

Gyorgy Sandor was born in Budapest, Hungary, and studied there at the Liszt Conservatory with Bartók (piano) and Kodály (composition). Mr. Sandor gave the first performance of Bartók's Piano Concerto No. 3 with Ormandy and the Philadelphia Orchestra in December, 1945. His recording of the entire piano repertory of Bartók won the Grand Prix du Disque. For Columbia and Vox, he has also recorded the complete solo piano works of Prokofiev and Kodály as well as works of Bach, Beethoven, Brahms, Chopin, Liszt, Rachmaninov, and Schumann.

Mr. Sandor concertizes annually in the United States, Europe, and Latin America, and has toured in Australia, the Far East, and North Africa.

Mr. Sandor is head of the doctoral program in piano performance at the University of Michigan.

Mr. Sandor, I'd like to know why you took a position in a university.

In my situation it was really a purely personal thing. I happened to concertize a great deal; I was on the road traveling eight to ten months a year. Since I was married and we had a little boy, I felt that I would like to have a place where he could be away from New York, where we then lived, and we could have a community where we could settle down, where I could return after tours and spend as much time as possible. So first of all, the motivation was a personal one.

Then professionally, of course, I certainly enjoyed the idea that I could pass on through teaching what I thought was good in music and piano-playing while continuing to concertize. At that time, when I settled in Dallas at Southern Methodist University, I got the dubious title of "artist-in-residence." It's still unclear what that means. For a performer, "artist-in-residence" is a contradiction. If you are "in residence," that means that you *reside* there and perform locally and you cease to be what we call an "artist" on the larger performing scene. So it really doesn't make much sense, and fortunately, I think most universities have dropped that title by now. It's very necessary that you be heard where you teach, but by no means should you give up traveling, if possible.

There is also the point of security. There is a certain income involved, a salary, which complements concertizing. The idea is that you can continue concertizing *with* the added security. We tend to forget after we settle at universities that the reason universities arranged to have us is because we *do* travel and concertize. When you settle somewhere there is a tendency to slow down and become part of the very attractive, very appealing university life. But the value of the performer is that universities have someone who carries the university's name around, who attracts good students nationally and internationally. If we stop concertizing, the university doesn't get its full value for what we were signed up for. One should manage to keep concertizing *and* teach at the university in order to fulfill one's complete role. If we don't, we not only do harm to ourselves but to the university as well. Some universities understand this and keep on encouraging our travels and concertizing.

Had you done any substantial teaching before going to Southern Methodist?

I did some, but not very much. Besides some private teaching which I did while I was still in Europe, I was head of the piano department at the Music Academy of the West in Santa Barbara for nine summers (if I remember well, from 1952 to 1961). So I did two months of teaching every year there. Otherwise, I did give some lectures and conferences in various universities—the University of Bogotá, the University of Mexico, and some other places.

As a matter of fact, I think there's one point we should clarify: practically every artist does some teaching and practically every teacher does some performing. One can't really draw a sharp line. Even Bach, Liszt, or Chopin—they all were teaching and performing at the same time.

In this country, a very wonderful thing happened: high-level music education was shifted from conservatories to universities. This is a unique thing; hopefully the rest of the world will follow us. It's a very healthy thing. It gives the student and the teacher the opportunity to live in a milieu where high-level intellectual activities are going on and the rather one-sided education which conservatories offer can be corrected. Conservatory students were trained in violin-playing, or piano-playing, and the like, and not really much else. Maybe some additional musical subjects, but not much else. So I thought this shift to universities was a very wonderful thing. I welcomed the idea of being with a university.

What have you enjoyed about the years you've spent in a university?

The feeling of belonging somewhere and being a part of a community is certainly a "plus." The student talent now is incredibly good—not only in this country but all over the world. The human population keeps increasing, so even if the percentage stays the same, the absolute number of exceptionally talented people increases. Most of these study music now at universities. I'm fortunate enough to work with very advanced students who are able to work on individual projects during my absences, and we work on the concert repertory which I play all the time.

By teaching you learn a great deal and it can be a very profitable experience. You work out problems which you have faced before through somebody else's difficulties. Sometimes you work something out intuitively—the way you feel it should be done. If you have difficulties, you try to analyze them, but most of the time you simply go through the material intuitively. But when you teach, you have to bring these things to the conscious level. You have to explain what goes on. For instance, if you play octaves you might not bother analyzing how you play them. You simply use them. When you teach, you have to go to the bottom of what this motion is like. How is it done? Where does the motion come from? By doing this kind of thinking you become aware of things in a way you weren't before.

When you interpret a phrase you may do it instinctively most of the time. If you have to explain, you'll find out that where you felt there should be emphasis, there may be a melodic or harmonic reason why that emphasis is needed. By analysis, you are turning the intuitive decisions to conscious ones. You learn.

When you consider the great amount of material your students play that you yourself have not actually studied or played, you learn by preparing the repertory with them. Here at Michigan we have a series where the graduate students do, for example, all the Debussy études, or Scriabin études, or Liszt études, or Prokofiev sonatas; well, a lot of this material you don't play yourself. On the other hand, even if you have a concerto you've played fifty times, sometimes students throw new light on it; sometimes interesting ideas that you hadn't had before come through. So teaching can be very enjoyable and profitable. A lot of people solve their own technical problems by analyzing them and trying to explain them to others.

All those things are positive. Now there are some things which aren't 100 percent right in university existence. On undergraduate levels, the role of the university is to disseminate as much knowledge about as many things as possible. When you go to higher-level education (from bachelor's to master's to doctoral level), then obviously the teaching ought to narrow to a certain extent simply because there is so much information, so much knowledge to be acquired that there is no time for one single person to know everything about everything. If you want to be *good* in a certain area, whether it's science or art, you will have to narrow somewhat your area of studies. If you are a pianist there is an immense repertory and immense amount of knowledge related to piano-playing. That in itself would occupy so much time that you wouldn't have time to do anything else. Now we want pianists to know something about other things too, but on the graduate level we have to realize that once you have a broad foundation in related areas such as theory, musicology, or sciences and other subjects unrelated to music, it's time to narrow things down. Certainly on the doctoral level! This obviously is done in engineering, chemistry, physics, and so on.

Is there something else which bothers you about university life?

There is a sort of general impression that the teaching profession hinders performance. I think it's a little bit less so now but in the past if you were attached to an educational institution people thought, "Well, he's no good anymore. He's changed careers." There was this superficial idea that anyone who was teaching was no longer a performer. Luckily this is changing. There was a kind of stigma in being in a college or university. But this is improving and hopefully will continue to improve. Someday we should be able to put on our concert publicity material that we are associated with such-and-such a university. At this point, it is of no advantage to do so. If you win a prize in some competition that seems to be a prestigious thing, although it's much less prestigious, I think, than if you teach in a university. Competitions are a dime a dozen now. I hope someday that situation will reverse itself: it ought to be more prestigious to be in a university teaching young artists.

What would be an ideal university situation for you?

The one I have now has many enjoyable aspects and certainly keeps on improving. If one could sum up what would make an ideal university, I believe it would be the one where the priorities are clearly defined and maintained. They vary, according to whether you are an undergraduate or graduate, whether you are in the research, music education, or performance fields. I would like to see musical values more thoroughly evaluated and established. We have problems with musical terminology: the same word may mean a totally different thing in one part of the country than in the other. I'd like to do away, also, with the obsession of creating new nomenclature for familiar old concepts.

Another significant deterioration in today's university activities is the excess of committees, subcommittees, ad hoc committees, and bureaucratic, administrative activities that are time-consuming and could be handled much better by trained administrators. Some of our best educators and specialists, composers and performers are overloaded with paperwork and meetings, at the expense of their primary duties: teaching and guiding the students.

One more preoccupation: in a democracy the duly elected representative can act responsibly. At universities certain specific projects—mostly on the higher level—are often interfered with by so-called "majority" votes. Fair as it seems to be, to have the continuous approval of every member of the faculty in every project is hardly possible. Control mechanisms other than "back reporting" are available and the person in charge should be trusted with his responsibilities. In many of these situations the numerical majority's votes will be misleading because of the majority's lack of information and expertise on that particular subject.

The main drawback about our cultural life and existence is an overall superficiality in most everything. Things are done in obvious ways. Complex and sophisticated questions are dealt with in capsule, instant fashion. "I like this. I don't like that." It's the *immediate* response which counts. This might be appropriate in popular literature, art, and journalism. In high-level scholarship and high-level art, it is *not* the obvious nor the immediate response which counts. No late Beethoven quartet or Bartók quartet was "liked" at first hearing.

How has affiliation with a university affected your career?

A professional performance career depends a great deal on factors such as management—good or bad—which is not related to university life. Successes or failures cannot be credited to or blamed on the university in any way. But if you don't have liberty to travel, obviously that is disadvantageous. Mobility is very important for a performer. I can't complain because here I have no difficulties getting away at any time.

Are you glad to be a university faculty member, all things considered?

I don't regret it for a moment. The university is a live organization and although it likes to resist sudden changes, it does progress. It is gratifying for me to see when "traditional" misconceptions are corrected and I try to do my share in this. I think the basic setup is ideal: universities are potentially wonderful things for art and for science. If you steer things the right way, progress can be spectacular.

Jason Seley

Jason Seley was born May 20, 1919, in Newark, New Jersey. After being graduated from Cornell, he studied with Ossip Zadkine at the Art Students League, and in Paris at the Ecole des Beaux-Arts.

In this country, important exposure of his work has occurred at the Guggenheim Museum, the Museum of Modern Art, the Whitney Museum, and many others. His sculptures also have received wide acclaim in many European exhibitions.

Mr. Seley teaches at Cornell University.

Mr. Seley, I'd like to talk with you about your dual roles as sculptor and professor.

The very first thought that comes to mind is, "How do they support each other?" There my immediate answer would be, "Association with young people." I find that association with young people keeps one's thinking alive and alert. They are the best critics in the world. I have always worked wherever I have taught. Here I only work on the campus, and when I am working on something the kids are very revealing, whether they try to be or not. If it bores them, I know it. If it turns them on, I know it. I trust the instinctive reactions of the young people far beyond that of the educated art critic in his middle years. They may not know why they feel something is great but they are very seldom wrong. At least I find this to be true. Being with young people keeps my thinking young and doesn't permit me to become complacent. When the brighter ones give me an argument about what I'm doing, sometimes the argument is based on some new ideas that have suddenly entered their minds. Sometimes, however, they are not finding some excitement in the work, some satisfaction in the work. At other times, they will come back and bring their friend: "Gee, look what Mr. Seley is turned on with." Then I know I'm hitting something vital and alive to them, and usually when that happens it is vital and alive in general. That has been my experience here and where I previously taught. I like to be around young minds for the benefit of my work.

I know many teachers find working with young people a draining experience. There are times when this can be true, but I, for the most part, have always found that I get as much as I give and this is the sort of thing that I find most beneficial to me. It's an exchange and for me it works.

The negative aspect, to answer the second part of your question, is that for the creatively involved individual, I do think that the average academic institution places considerable demands on one's time and you don't have enough time for your work—at least that's my feeling. I'm not referring to just the teaching load as such. If one is just a teacher and teaches his courses and that's all, it's really not a bad situation. But somehow if you're with an institution and you're responsible, you get involved. Then there are meetings and committees and all sorts of garbage that impose terribly on one's time.

Would you rate that as a big concern?

Oh sure. I would definitely say so. I like college teaching. I would like to stay in college teaching. I like the exchange I have with the students enormously. I would like to be spending about half as much time as I actually do.

Have you been able to change the direction of this department?

There has been a greater liberalization of the curriculum than existed when I came here, so I think from the students' point of view, it's a much more wide-open situation than it was three years ago in terms of requirements to complete an undergraduate degree.

Why did you want to do that?

Well, I rather strongly feel that the situation that I came to (which was that a student had to specialize in either painting, sculpture, or graphics) was less in tune with the times than it was some years ago. I wanted a situation where the student could cross boundaries much more easily and still have the necessary requirements for a degree.

Let's talk some more about you. You were talking about satisfactions and dissatisfactions as an artist-teacher in the university. Are there more things you would like to explore along these lines?

Let's put it this way: there are in this country and in any country very, very few artists who can be self-supporting just on the basis of their art, and I'm not one of them. Now if I have to supplement my income, I can't think of a nicer way to do it than as a member of a university faculty. It's a healthy, good, intellectually alert community. Associations are very enjoyable. The life-style is very satisfactory to me. I just think it's the best solution for me.

If I were independently wealthy and did not have to teach, or if I made enough money from my work so that I did not have to teach, I would still choose to do so, but I would choose, at most, the equivalent of half-time. I would definitely choose to remain with this or some other university. But I would like to just teach one course, just to maintain an association which for me is a great pleasure and very satisfying. As I said at the very outset, I find it very helpful in my self-realization.

Do you like to teach all students?

I suspect that (without ever really giving it too much thought) I do, because before I ever got into college teaching, I taught in Haiti for several years in an art center there. That was volunteer: I didn't get paid at all. In most of the jobs I have had, I have usually ended up with some kind of a role where a lot of my work was training less experienced people, and I guess I always kind of enjoyed it. I've done it most of my life so I guess I really do enjoy it.

Do you think one needs a certain critical mass of fellow artists on a faculty?

As far as I'm concerned, that is unimportant to me. I do think that at a certain stage in an artist's development he must be exposed to this kind of a critical mass. I think that's probably what I miss most about New York City. But as far as having to have such a group with me on a given faculty, no, I think that's relatively unimportant. I say that because I have been on faculties when there have not been such people and I have been perfectly comfortable there.

Maybe that's not entirely true: I used to hang out with the composers at Hofstra. I was always with the music department people and I guess I was making an overstatement just now. I realize that, now that I have stopped and given it some thought. I guess I have never been in the situation where there haven't been artists around. In Haiti there were a great number of absolutely fascinating artists around, not of the same type that one thinks of in the general Western sense. They were primitive artists, but it didn't make them any less artists. At Hofstra, there were times when our own art department was very weak in people with a real creative drive and commitment. As I mentioned, I was always hanging around with the composers, who did seem to have more of that, so I guess I would be uncomfortable lacking that. I have probably never been in a position where I lacked that.

Would you go to a position like that knowing now what you know?
I don't think so. When Cornell asked me to come up here, I remember, I said to my wife, "It is the only position outside of New York that I would have even considered." I had several offers over the years that were economically better than the situation I found myself in in New York. I never accepted.

You said you get some kind of stimulation from students.
Right, absolutely. I feel the instinctive taste-drive of the young. I am not restricting it to a high-caliber art major, just any young people who are of college age. They are usually in some form of art. The theater kids at Hofstra were as rewarding, or the music majors were as rewarding to be with as the art students. They didn't have to be art students.

I tend to be very easygoing and very libertarian. I have never been convinced that you can teach a person to be an artist. He either is or he isn't. You can put him through a number of courses and he may still go back into daddy's business or become a Westchester gentleman, or something else, you know. You can't teach a person to be an artist but I like to think you can recognize it when you find it in the mind, when you see it near you. I am afraid that a lot of people don't hold my view.

What kind of people don't?

There are many people who believe that you can put a student through a number of training paces and thereby produce an artist. I don't believe that. I tend to think that the student is working when he is just thinking and being troubled and being puzzled. I tend to think that if he concentrates all his efforts in one enthusiastic area of interest to the neglect of other areas of interest this is perfectly healthy, but a lot of people don't feel that way; and not only don't they feel that way in the character of the overall curriculum but in the character of the way they conduct their own courses, so I see a high percentage of dropouts among our students. In many cases they are the good ones, and I am very frustrated by this but I don't know how to handle it. I'll usually side with the student.

But let me ask you to clarify something. If an artist either is or is not, what role does this faculty play?

Well, this has to go back to an earlier answer. I think he will be a better person, he will lead a better life, if he has as broad a college education as possible at the same time that his primary interests receive sufficient engagement. That's why I like our B.F.A. curriculum as it now stands, which permits a lot of work in the department so that the student stays engaged with his major interests at the same time that he learns other things that are going to add to his life enjoyment—music courses or a knowledge of history or whatever it may be. I'm also convinced that a person with a college degree is going to fare better in life economically and walk into fewer frustrations toward achieving his artistic goals. I know this has been true in my case.

It was during the time I was in college that I decided I wanted to be an artist. I wanted to quit school immediately, go to the Art Students League, and just be a sculptor. But a lot of wiser heads (I now recognize them to be wiser heads; I didn't think so at the time) said, "Get your degree." Well I did, and I found all through life that jobs were easier to find when I needed them because I was a college graduate (not that I had one damn qualification more because I was a college graduate but companies thought I did, you know). I have gotten fellowships for which I would not even have been eligible to apply without at least a bachelor's degree. I lived in Haiti for three and a half years; two years of it was on a fellowship that I would not have been able to apply for had I not had the B.A. I had a Fulbright. How can you get a Fulbright without a B.A.?

So I really have argued with a lot of kids, saying, "Get your degree, I mean it's not all that hard, it's not all that bad, it's not all that frustrating. Get your degree. Just postpone your life in the loft in the city for another eighteen months and stick it out, because somewhere along the line later, it's going to make life easier for you."

If I had a school of art somewhere, and absolute power at my disposal to mold for you a position and an academic milieu that would be ideal for you, what would I need to have in that school?

Well, you would have to have a lot of physical space for my work and my students' work—preferably an old informal kind of a building. You would have to have a curriculum that would give the students many very liberal options so that if they just wanted to work on sculpture, they could, and if in working on sculpture some of them wanted to work together rather than as individuals, that would have to be allowed. If some of them wanted to work with or for me, that would have to be allowed. I guess that's it, fundamentally. When you say mold a school for me, I think of myself as a sculptor and of my situation in it.

You're confusing me, because earlier you were giving some lip service to liberal education and now you are saying that in my utopian school students would have to be allowed to do only sculpture if that's what they cared to do. What's the crucial variable?

I would say the crucial variable is whether the student wishes himself to be a degree candidate or doesn't care about it.

I feel that my best education came when I was a student at the Art Students League after college. But I also feel that there is a lot to be gained from a college education.

But I am still trying to figure out how much of your commitment to the so-called liberal education course available here is a kind of pro forma commitment to what a degree implies and how much is really a personal gut feeling of your own.

I don't really know that I know the answer to that myself. I like the idea of a college education. I think it should have, within certain liberal requirements, enormous variables that distinguish one student from another. I guess that's it.

Has anything happened to your own creative output as a result of university affiliation?

A great deal has happened. My whole approach has changed enormously, and now, of course, we are getting down to the problem of the chairmanship. You saw what I was working on in my studio—I've been working on that for almost two years. The first year I was here, I got almost no work done and I realized I had moved into a totally different life rhythm by being the chairman and I just never had any free time, or when I had the free time I didn't have a free mind. My older way of working just didn't happen anymore. That was very contemplative work, and a thing that looked to be done in a half-hour or, well, a week sometimes took six months and a lot of going back and forth and quiet thought and solitude. I just found myself "out" as far as that was concerned. The first year I was here I did some constructivist things from previous ideas; in other words, the whole idea was conceived on paper and then constructed, but that really isn't my direction. So at the end of the first year, I was really feeling quite desperate, you know. "How do I get out of this chairmanship now?" or "Am I presiding over my own artistic suicide?" I decided, "Well, you had an idea several years ago and you never did anything about it because it seemed like too big an idea, but maybe this is the time to do it. Give yourself a big ambitious project where the nature of the work is such that you can drop it or pick it up where you left it, at any given time." The idea that I had had back about 1964 that I had never done anything about was to do a new version of the equestrian statue of Colleoni by Verrocchio. So I said to myself, "Well, now is the time to do it," and it has worked beautifully.

Does it seem easier to you to leave off and then pick up where you were before on a great big piece of work?

It's not the bigness of it. It's the fact that it's sort of an aesthetic, intellectual jigsaw puzzle, if you stop and think about it. I am not making the same kind of aesthetic determinations when I am reinterpreting someone else's work that I would be making if I were working in a free associative way. I have a problem. I know what the forms are. I know what the dimensions are. I know what the composition is. My problem is to reinterpret it with my materials, which I have worked with for many years. In a sense, I just create a huge puzzle for myself and then proceed to solve the puzzle, and I can literally walk away and come back to that with almost no sense of interruption. I was in Germany for seven months last year and I came back and the next day I was able to walk in the studio and pick up right where I left off.

Is the difference in the level of creativity that you have to bring to bear on what you are doing?

I don't know that "level" is the word; it's the type of creativity. It's a different type of creativity. My other, older work has always been made without me knowing what I was making. I never started with an idea that "I'm going to make sculpture of a certain type." They've happened as I have worked on them. It's always been a kind of free-association action sculpture as compared to action painting, where the artist starts to slash around on a canvas with a brush and this suggests something and then he does something else and that suggests something so he does something else again.

But he doesn't know before he starts where he is going to end. Well, that's the way I have always made my sculptures and this requires a kind of disciplined peace and quiet, in a sense. I mean peace and quiet of the inner mind, to afford the luxury of working that way. Now when I found I couldn't do this, I felt that I was setting myself a project where the limits were known, and within that I could work and function very well, so I have been working on this particular statue for a year and a half. It normally could have been done in about a year. If I could do a piece like that in a year while being chairman, I feel that I've solved the problem very nicely. After all, it took Verrocchio about five and a half years and he hadn't finished it when he died.

I'm sorry to keep harping on this but I'm trying to understand how your own goals could be related to those of the university. The university is supposed to teach, but you say artists are not made, they're born.

Probably I'm not that straight in my own mind about it. I think in our society in the twentieth century, the person with the college education has a better chance for self-realization, whether it is in engineering or arts. For instance, look at the artists of the period of the 1920s and the 1930s. Not a one of them had a college education, and they didn't need it. It wasn't part of the pattern of that period. But if you look at the significant artists of today, it's incredible the large number of them that are college-educated people. You see, we've moved into a different era.

When I was a sophomore, I had taken a required course in sculpture for architectural students and that changed my life. I was a very conventional sculptor. Then I got out of school just before World War II. I wasn't in the army but I was involved, naturally, with war work so we were all working sixty- to seventy-hour weeks in those days and it wasn't until 1943 that I had a job that didn't require night work as well as day work. So my entire sculpture training really was at the Art Students League at night after a full day's work. I directed my whole life to accomplish this. In other words, I managed to get a job that was only four blocks from the Art Students League and managed to find an apartment that was only three blocks in the other direction so that I would literally have the physical time to go to the league for three hours every night of the week and I did that for about two years. That's where I really studied sculpture. But the world we live in today has no use for an artist or anyone else on the job market at the age of seventeen or eighteen, for crying out loud, and why can't *all* young people have a college education prior to specialization, to open the doors of their minds, you know, to music, to literature, to all of these things, and then specialize. I didn't want to do it at the time. I wanted to just get up and leave, but I am so glad in retrospect that it happened the other way.

You have said time is a big problem for you at this point. But you have also said that's because you are chairman of the department. Do you think that other faculty members here have a much better edge time-wise than you do?

Sure. When I was asked to come to Cornell, as I said, the only way that I could come here was as chairman, because all the people here were sensible enough to not want to take the job. I didn't like it where I was so I told Cornell I could come—but not for a year. I quit a year ahead of time and just took a year off because I was in a position to do it at that time. I am very glad I did. During that one-year period, I took a ten-week assignment as artist-in-residence at Dartmouth, but apart from that it was a great year to work in my own studio.

Why didn't you like it where you were before the residency at Dartmouth?

I didn't like the department. I didn't like the art education mentality, I didn't like the standpoint of the deans and things like that. It was a school of education, you know; and it was just outrageous in terms of space. What these kids had to put up with was ghastly. I taught sculpture in a room not quite twice the size of this room and I had four courses a week, and that room was used for three or four other courses a week in sculpture or three-dimensional design. Each course had about fifteen students in it, so you can get an idea of the traffic, with all their work and all their storage of materials and everything in that one room.

They must have done very small pieces.
They certainly did. Very small pieces. I mean it was outrageous in terms of space limitation. It just drove me up the wall.

I think I now have another picture of you; it's slowly developing into better shape. You say that you like to teach all students but you really don't mean it because you don't like to teach uncommitted, ungifted students, is that right?
I guess it's better the other way. Sure. Naturally, it's better the other way. But I thought I'd made the point clear, that I never had any objection to the students at that other school. It was the faculty and the administration and the physical space.

OK. What was wrong with the faculty there?
Well, first of all you have to understand that I was the only one on that faculty (I mean the permanent, tenured faculty) who didn't have a Ph.D.

I don't know exactly what that says.
You don't? I think it says a great deal.

Were they artists or were they scholars?
In most cases they were neither. They were people who had done sufficient scholarship to ensure themselves a comfortable position and claimed to be artists. In one case the man was a genuine artist, but he kept the fact that he had a Ph.D. a secret. Very few people knew it. He really was an artist. Why and at what period in his life he felt that he had to get his Ph.D. for security reasons, I don't know. But most of the others believed in

some kind of a dogma of art education, and you know, I could sit in faculty meetings for weeks on end and not say a word because I had nothing to say to these people. The reasoning was just in a different world. It just had nothing to do with me or with what I was trying to teach and with what the students wanted to learn. This was a joke to the students, too. They wanted teaching degrees so they could teach and find security that way but they used to refer to courses as "Window Shade Raising IV" and "Clean the Erasers IIB." It was a joke to them, and a lot of them were very good and committed students who wanted to be artists, or wanted to be teachers for very good reasons.

Would you say that one of the reasons you felt so alienated from this faculty was that they were not aesthetically alive?

No. They were hypocrites! They really thought they were teaching art. They really thought that they were a good art department. They honestly believed that they were training young artists and they weren't.

In what ways were they not?

First of all, the teaching was as much on the graduate level as the undergraduate level, and what would get approved as a thesis as opposed to what a student might want to do became so much crap. At the same time, these people would give lip service to the fact that they were training young artists. They kept talking about "research" all the time and I would every once in a while say, "Why don't you talk about search for a change and forget research? Let's just talk about search." They would look at me as if I had mentioned a dirty word. I think they didn't themselves know how dishonest they were.

What repels a creative, producing artist from a university faculty? You appear to be very happy here in lots of ways and you seemed to be so miserable there, I want to understand the diffference.

Well, what is the difference here? We do not have art education. We do not have art history. You will not find a single "craft" course in this department. You will not find an art education course in this department. It is a department of all studio courses taught by all studio people. There is not a person in this department who is not an artist, and while we may cover a tremendous spectrum of differences in what we feel about art, we all have the same prejudices about certain other things.

This former faculty fascinates me. Were they just insensitive boobs? I don't quite understand why being a doctorate-holder and an art educator precludes being a sensitive artist.

I don't say that it precludes it; I think it is not likely to happen.

And so it's the Ph.D.-holder and the art educator: he's the man you don't have much sympathy, patience, or respect for?

I guess that's correct. Yes.

Why?

It's because he thinks he knows what art is, and by God he hasn't got the faintest idea in the world. That's the bone of contention! The son-of-a-bitch thinks he knows what art is and he's much more verbal than I am, you know, because he's a verbal type to begin with (which I'm not), and he's telling me all about art. It's just Chinese; it's a different language.

OK. I think I now know what you mean.

Seymour Shifrin

Seymour Shifrin was born in New York City on February 28, 1926. He was educated at Columbia (A.B., M.A.). His teachers in composition included William Schuman, Otto Luening, and Darius Milhaud. He received the Copley Award, the Boston Symphony Orchestra Horblit Award, and Fulbright and Guggenheim fellowships.

His "Satires of Circumstance" received the Koussevitzky International Recording Award for 1970. "Three Pieces for Orchestra" won the Naumburg Award; a recording of this work also won the Koussevitzky Award for 1972. He has fulfilled commissions from the Juilliard School of Music, the University of Michigan, the International Society for Contemporary Music, and the Koussevitzky Foundation of the Library of Congress, as well as from various performers and publishers.

Mr. Shifrin teaches at Brandeis University.

We should talk about the duality in your present career. You are a composer and professor of music. They are related but different, and that will be the focus of what we will talk about. I would like to know what factors influenced your decision to teach in a university.

That is difficult in the sense that I hope to be perfecty frank in my response although one never knows. I suppose as much as anything, it was the sense that the alternatives did not loom large to begin with. A composer lives somewhat on the fringe of his society if he can be said to live in society at all *as composer.* There are very few of us who find a way to subsist apart from one form of teaching or another, but if I left it at that, that wouldn't be quite frank with you either, because teaching does interest me; I give a good deal of my energies to the enterprise. Over the years, whatever may have happened to my students, I think I have learned something that has been both relevant to my work and satisfying beyond that. But I don't know if that answers your question or not. Principally, it seemed like the way of life that would afford me the degree of privacy that I would need for my work so that I would be my own man, that I could do the music I wanted to do and pursue the interests that I had without any kind of pressure of an economic nature. In a way, as it comes from my mouth, that's a ludicrous thing for a composer to say, because ideally he should be writing music that would be wanted and heard as soon as the ink was dry on the page, but little of that is known today. Few of us experience that kind of relationship with a public—let alone a group of performers. Given that fact, the university affords us the possibility of pursuing our interests fully and intensely when we can find the time, but at least there is no sense of pleasing anyone but our friends and ourselves.

You said the university could afford you the privacy *to do that. I'm not sure I understood perfectly your use of that word.*

Well, I enjoy the sense of intense secrecy. Composition is to some degree not a public act, certainly not at the time of composition. If it ever becomes a public act, it is after the fact. At the time of performance, then of course it changes in nature, but the enterprise of composition itself is for me an intensely private act. I have to find the time and the isolation. At the university, generally, it has been possible for me to arrange things just that way. You have come to me at the end of a rather poor year. Somehow or other, this year has been particularly difficult and my arrangements haven't quite worked out the way they normally would and I've had relatively little time to do my work. I hope to remedy that this summer.

I hope so too. You said that you like to teach. Would you talk a little more about that? Why? What's so great about teaching?

There is something profoundly rewarding in stimulating in the mind and ear of another person excitement about a piece, or the kind of excitement that comes from an insight of a student composer into his own work—something that perhaps he hadn't quite realized about a potential in his own music or the way a given work relates its parts to a whole. To the degree that

that communicates—and it doesn't communicate all that often—one is rewarded in teaching.

How do you know when you've done that?

He then perhaps can do something that he hadn't been capable of before. It's in the doing, utimately, that I know. Also, in
some subtle way, his standards *change* to some degree. He becomes more restless, more dissatisfied with the commonplace
or at least what had been the commonplace for him up to that
point.

It's no great favor I do him if this, in fact, happens. But it's
the proper sort of pain that one suffers. There's pain and there's
pain.

*What have been your principal satisfactions, apart from teaching,
and what have been some of the frustrations of your dual role?*

Well, I'll take the latter first. Frustrations, I suppose, come
from sounding like a moralist at times, not necessarily meaning
to. There is so much that is involved in composition that has to
do with the quality of not fooling oneself, a kind of severe ability to see one's self and one's work as it is, not to be satisfied
with the possible but to go beyond what the work really seems
to permit in the way of continuation. There's an important and
often vast distinction between what is plausible as a possibility
and what is better than plausible. That's something you can't
teach. Either the student has that quality in the end or he
doesn't. You can tell him how important it is and that's when
you touch on dangerous ground, I suppose. You can sound very
pompous and moralistic at such a moment. But the profound
frustrations in teaching student composers often come from the
fact that some of them seem superbly equipped, marvelously
equipped, but lack a certain quality of character to see an issue
through beyond what they can do off the top of their head, and
that is very frustrating indeed. The satisfactions come, con-
trariwise, when someone stretches beyond his seeming capacity to find something to hold on to beyond what he was capable
of before. That kind of an effort is crucial to any kind of achieve-

ment—to go beyond what you seemed to be capable of. There's an analogy, perhaps, to the long-distance runner. He knows that he trains for that. He trains to *go beyond.* In some sense, that has to come into the training of both performer and composer as well, it seems to me.

Has university life stood in your way somehow?
Not actively, not purposefully; occasionally stupidly, as if it were unaware—not "as if," but probably thoroughly unaware—that I exist apart from my role as teacher. Generally there's been not overwhelming awareness of the fact that I compose and that that might be of interest. I find it troubling that a community of scholars, of the cultural elite, would not find it within their purview to be curious and even seeking to know what is happening in the arts. It seems to be both respectable and forgivable to dismiss current activity, which seems to me a shocking attitude.

Are you talking about the university faculty as a whole or are you talking about your colleagues in this department?
The university faculty as a whole. It seems to me that not too long ago, maybe as much as just a century ago but perhaps not even as long as that, the ability to play an instrument would have fallen within the common definition of what it is to be a cultured man. That would certainly have involved him in reading the latest music available. It would certainly have involved his going to concerts to hear what was happening in the way of most recent music. It would have been something that perhaps he would look forward to and he might well have considered it a failing if he did not know what was happening. The curious thing is that the interest seems to be there in the plastic arts; it doesn't extend, at the moment, to music for some strange reason. I'm not sure why.

At the University of California at Berkeley, where I spent fourteen years before coming to Brandeis, there were few but notable occasions when I heard my work. As a young man, it was crucial that I heard my work. Still and all, I think it is something of a blot on somebody's landscape (primarily my own I suppose) that I can't say that I have heard *all* my work by any means and that I was obliged to wait years in the case of some of my work. I think the university should be a little more hospitable that way. At Brandeis we make a point of trying to play all our students' music as soon as possible so that they have the opportunity of hearing what they are doing at an early moment, and I think that is not simply an obligation but a source of stimulation to the faculty as well.

Well, let's talk about the good things then. That's a little more fun anyhow. Besides teaching, are there other things which have proven to be rewarding?

Apart from the inevitable dosage of pompous asses, I find many of my colleagues stimulating. I have had long and close friendships with people outside of my department as well as people in the department and I value this. That's not to say they are my only friends by any means, but certainly they have been important friendships for me.

However, I am aware of a kind of uneasy truce at times. They are not quite sure; they're somewhat suspicious of the enterprise of the arts in the curriculum of the university. They are not quite sure about what it represents. I think I've indicated to you that I don't mean to prove to them the rigor involved in the study of music. I think it is as demanding a rigor as any I can imagine. And actually, in talking to some of my scientist friends I find certain analogies in attitude between their creative work and ours. The differences are also profound. They do have recourse to a proof; we don't.

What do you think has happened to your own creative output as a result of university affiliation?

Again, it's hard to be honest in response to that. I think I would be honest in saying that it has been somewhat curtailed. Had I had more time, I would have had more work to show for it. I think while I do enjoy and do profit from my association with the university and with my students, I also think I am one of those birds that could occupy a lifetime with my work and not be unhappy for it. I have spoken to many colleagues who feel that their teaching acts as a counterfoil and in that way, to some degree, they are permitted to escape the difficulties of their work, and that in the end allows time to come back refreshed perhaps or with new energy. I would love to have a protracted period of trial and unrelieved work.

What are you trying to accomplish with students here?

A student has come to the university, hopefully, meaningfully in distinction to a conservatory or even a school of music. What could that possibly mean as a choice? It must mean that he wants to avail himself of what there might be at a university in contrast to a professional school. That is, he would want to do work in the sciences, he would want to do something in language, he might want to do something in philosophy, he might want to do something in literature; all these things might be of interest to him.

Only some of them intend a professional life in music. Others are devoted to music but perhaps to some degree their love is unrequited. They can go so far but they don't in all honesty entertain any hopes of a professional career in music. They are students of music and that's quite respectable! They want to know as much as they possibly can. Some of them, because of the range of their interest, might well go on to professional work in history, in musicology. We want to train them to be different historians from some of the historians in the past. We want them to be in a position to make sound judgments about the music they are studying, not indiscriminate judgments, not purely statistical judgments, but judgments that have to do with the workings of a piece.

Frankly, I think of a composer as a kind of aristocrat in a special sense (not to the manner born): someone who is not easily pushed around mentally or physically, and in the service of his not being pushed around mentally, he needs to be trained and he needs to seek information and stimulation from whatever source. There's good reason for him to be at a university, but I can't imagine a composer's training starting at the university in music. If in fact it does, I think the chances are very slim that he'll succeed. However, given the fact that he started his musical training back there somewhere at the tender age of four or five, then I think the time he spends in his courses apart from music may well be time well spent.

What are some ways universities could improve conditions under which artists work?

If the university were really interested in the breed and valued the breed, it might be possible to establish another way of life, perhaps a kind of preserve. Now this might make trouble with other colleagues. I don't know, but hopefully it wouldn't. Given a responsible, committed teacher-composer, it should be possible to allow him to make certain critical decisions. That is, this year I teach; the next term I've got something cooking in the way of a large project, so I would like a reduced load. Perhaps I make it up the following term. Something that would permit his particular value to the institution to come to the fore. Supposing he becomes interested in arranging a series of performances; I don't see why that couldn't be considered a service to the university—that he involved himself with students in the preparation of a series of pieces for performance. The next term or the next year, he may see his duties differently. There should be flexibility to avail the university and its students of his contributions and allow him discretion in deciding what would be best to do at any given time. I think it should be extended to all university faculties. It may make some problems in scheduling but maybe some clever administrator could find a way of reconciling the schedule with the fact that there are individuals involved.

Well, some clever or not so clever administrator would ask you in a situation like that, "What is the university going to get out of this deal anyway?" If you create a preserve for the breed and the composer goes off to this preserve and composes music, what does the university realize out of the deal? Why should the university pay you a salary to compose music? They pay you a salary to teach music.

Well, just as somehow or other the university has come to the point where it recognizes the importance of giving the scientist his laboratory and time for research as *part of his work* at the university (I suppose on the theory that what he would then achieve would be a direct contribution to knowledge and since the general enterprise has to do with knowledge and skill and accomplishment in general), I think there would be a direct bearing on supporting the composer perhaps for part of his stay at the university in his principal activity. There is that analogy. Beyond that, it's the sort of thing that in the end teaches him most, and insofar as he is to grow and the university is not to be a source of frustration to him but is to allow him the possibility of growth and expansion of his potential, it would be pertinent to encourage those activities.

Imagine I'm trying to hire you away from Brandeis University. What would an attractive position be? What would it need to have to get you away from this institution?

I think you led me there very gracefully. I think I have more or less described the circumstances that I would consider both reasonable and ideal in which to work: where I am treated as a responsible member of a community that has work to do, and where my judgment would be respected as to whether my contribution at this particular time would best be in the service of my work or in the service of organizing a group of concerts of music that hadn't been heard locally before and certainly with students who hadn't played that music before, or whether it would be some combination of that with teaching or purely teaching. One activity would be more welcome than another or more appropriate to my interest at the time.

What kind of students would this utopia have?

Few and hand-picked. Ideally, again, it would be a world where no one would be obliged to study with me and conversely I would not be obliged to study with them. We would be self-selected on both sides.

What about administrators?

The administrator would be that paragon of virtue sympathetic to all sides, all complaints, and somehow capable of finding a way out of the muddle. Lord help the administrator. I don't know. I think he must have clearly in mind what the enterprise is all about and from time to time remind the participants as well, because they forget. I think I have had rather curious responses at times when I have stopped a class and said, "What are we doing this for? What possible reason, what possible bearing can the realization of this exercise (or whatever it is) have on your life? Why are you studying music in a larger sense and more particularly why are you in this class? What do you hope to gain?" If an administrator can create an atmosphere where it remains reasonably clear why people are there, both students and teachers as well as administrators, then he has fulfilled his function brilliantly, I would say.

Do you measure the value of an activity by its popularity? If the answer is "Oh yes," then of course there is no reason for the university to support music or any of the other arts. If, on the other hand, there is something about the activity itself that is thought to represent one of man's finest, even the recalcitrant kind of people who couldn't care less give a grudging respect to the enterprise. It's a puzzling thing, you know; why should music be considered among the best achievements of man? It does represent the kind of achievement that is in fact the best that a talented man can do. I think that doesn't escape an attentive and perceptive listener. It is in the end an act of conscience to set down not what is possible but *beyond* what was thought to be possible—to delve beyond possibility as it had been defined up to that point.

The crisis in music extends not only to contemporary music; somehow there is something a little musty about our public music-making institutions. Part of it, I think, has to do with so much of musical experience for the general public being more and more secondhand—turning on a switch and not making it for themselves, not singing in a chorus, not singing even in the church choir, or the local orchestra or the weekly chamber group or the nightly singing around the piano by a family. It's become more and more a spectator sport and music as a whole has suffered for it.

If I had to say Seymour Shifrin is happy or unhappy in the university as an artist-teacher, I'm not sure what I would say.

Well, I would place it right smack in between. I think I am both happy and unhappy. I think a state of tension is the best way to describe my existence, and for that matter, so long as that state of tension is a meaningful one, so long as the pulls are reasonable and are ones that I can manage and are in directions that interest me, then I am willing to live with that state of tension.

Jack Squier

Jack Squier was born in Dixon, Illinois, February 27, 1927. He studied at Indiana University (B.S.) and Cornell (M.F.A.). He has since 1965 been a member of the International Association of Art (UNESCO), and has been vice-president of that international body since 1970.

His sculptures have been exhibited in numerous one-man shows in New York City, at Cornell University, and in Lima, Peru. His work has been included in frequent group showings at centers such as the Art Institute of Chicago, the Los Angeles County Museum of Art, and internationally. Among others, the Museum of Modern Art and the Whitney Museum hold his works in their collections.

Mr. Squier teaches at Cornell University.

Mr. Squier, what factors persuaded you to become a faculty member?

Only an involved answer, I suppose, will do here. I think generally, most practicing artists in this country and in most countries teach primarily because it's a way of making a living doing what they do best. It's very simple. There are a lot of people who truly like to teach and a lot who don't. I enjoy teaching (with the exception of the last year or so when we have had the student unrest, which has simmered down almost totally now as far as any classroom resistance is concerned). It's just a great deal of fun partly because one learns all the time. I think it was Xenophon who said something to the effect that he saw no difference between teaching and studying as long as it was his subject. He didn't mind either way and I don't either. For example, this summer I am involved in working with realistic human figures, and I've gone out of my way to teach a six-week class two hours a day from the nude model, because I need the practice. I wasn't even planning to teach until this possibility came up, so this will give me two hours a day of critical work helping people work from the model. I haven't worked from the model in quite a few years and I am sharpening up my own interest. I will be paid for doing exactly what I like to do, and I will be learning. So I like teaching. I would teach even if I didn't have to.

Would you really?

Some of the time, at least to have some contact with serious graduate students anyway.

How long have you been at Cornell?

Since 1958. I got a graduate degree here in 1950 and I taught then as a teaching assistant. I lived in New York for about six years and I came back in 1958. I taught in Berkeley one summer, and when I was very young—just out of school—I taught up in Maine at a summer art school for two or three summers just to have a place to live.

Do you like teaching generally, or do you like teaching just some students?

I wouldn't care a damn to teach in a school that had indifferent students. It's all involved with sculpture. I like sculpture, I like people who like sculpture, and I'm an older sculptor, and I am very pleased to pass on things to younger sculptors as they were passed on to me by older sculptors. If I had to teach in a school that was full of indifferent students, I'd rather build houses for a living because I have done that and that's fun too. So the kind of student definitely has a lot to do with it.

By "indifferent" do you mean nonprofessional?

No. Stupid, indifferent, just insensitive. I have had very good, interesting students who were nonprofessional. As a matter of fact, we very often recruit people into our field from the rest of the university, lots of good students who have been engineers, architects, just general humanists and so forth who have decided to do graduate work in painting or sculpture. I myself had that sort of undergraduate education: pre-engineering and business and public administration.

It's easy to teach very gifted students and it's easy to love teaching under that circumstance.

Sure, it's easy to teach, but only in the way it's easy to play a fine instrument. Why not have everything really good? Nothing is too good for art and artists.

The nonsense for the last few years made it utter hell. As a matter of fact, it got so bad around here that I went abroad about four times in the last two years just to get away. I had the opportunity and the students were absolutely preoccupied and no pleasure at all. Now they are back at work, so it's rather encouraging. I think I'll stay.

As a sculptor in the university, what have been some of your concerns, dissatisfactions, maybe even frustrations, if that's not too strong a word?

Well, my answer may surprise you. I think that by and large (and I'm not speaking for all artists and all universities but I am speaking for myself at Cornell, and some of my colleagues too, I think), this is a fantastically wonderful arrangement for an artist. You're looking at a happy man. I'm not frustrated, I'm not unhappy. I feel no pressures. I'm on a first-name basis with the president. The high-ranking officials in the university buy people's drawings and prints. We're building a beautiful new art museum designed by I. M. Pei. Very possibly a tremendous collection is coming to it. I'm given this studio to work in, janitor service, electricity, power tools. I'm expected to work. This department is full of practicing artists, nobody else. Nobody has ever been invited to join the staff who isn't an active, practicing, exhibiting artist. It's a busy, nifty environment and there are creative artists all over the place. There are good musicians, poets, the scientists tend to be equally as interesting; sort of brethren, you know, searching out stuff that isn't specifically traditional academic work. There are a couple thousand people on this campus who by and large are all interested in the arts. I think you could not find anybody who had a feeling of hostility toward the arts except (and I'm saying this only half as a joke) art historians. There always is that funny feeling that they have about having living artists around. David Smith, the sculptor, was asked about the importance of art historians—what was the relationship and what was the importance of the art historian to the artist? He said, "Of the same importance as ornithologists are to birds." It's a very friendly atmosphere and so I am completely contented in all these areas.

I know other people who are not contented. The only reason to be frustrated is if you're in some kind of personal difficulty yourself. The university can't really do any more for anybody than they do for us. They could pay us more money but everybody could pay everybody more money.

I can't get you to gripe about anything?

I'll endlessly gripe about things that I think are worth griping about. If it's true that I can't find anything to gripe about, I should think that's refreshing. One finds endlessly in New York papers and magazines (you know all these headache journals that we all torture ourselves with reading every day) all these awful things about the university. Largely it's crap. It's written by frustrated people who, for one reason or another, never learned how to function within a university. Universities are heaven on earth for intellectuals who have any goodwill at all. We just lost a great sorehead—a sociologist who writes endlessly for public consumption. He really saw Ithaca and Cornell as some kind of hell on earth, you know. If you didn't know what he was talking about, or didn't know him, you could imagine that he either had wandered by accident into a state mental institution or had just been dumped in a jail on the Isle of Pines in Cuba or something like that. But these guys are always getting published. Nobody with any reasonable feelings of satisfaction about the university can write a very interesting article about it. People who are reasonably satisfied with their own work don't go around writing articles. They work.

What has happened to your work as a result of university affiliation? Does it seem to you that things might have been different if you hadn't had a certain commitment and responsibility to the university as a teacher?

I lived in Manhattan for six years right after I got out of school, when I was in my twenties, and had to carry on a full-time job and work evenings and weekends. I guess something would have happened; I wouldn't have done nearly as much work for one thing. I would have been working to make a living at something unrelated to my medium. It never helps—the crap and the myth that hungry artists make better artists. Distracted artists don't make better artists. Artists who have to get silly jobs in order to support themselves don't make better artists. They make worse artists because they don't have time to think about it. I think that to be anything like an effective artist you've got to have this drumming in the back of your head all the time. When you're sitting in a dentist's office, what do you think about? When you're driving down the road, what do you think about? Not some nagging money worry or how you sneak into the neighbor's wife's bedroom. Your work should be on your mind and it can't be on your mind if you are plagued by money troubles and political troubles. I think the university has made it possible for me and a lot of artists in my generation to function and produce and experiment without fear of loss of sales of work and things like that.

I'm changing from having been an abstract artist all my life. What reputation I might have is all connected with that work. Now I'm doing total realism and I'm determined to give it about two years. If it works out, fine. If not, it's been a great lesson and I'll be a much better teacher of human figures if nothing else because I'm really learning a lot. But I intend now to try something I've never really tried before: to be an artist in historical context. Not to be able to do this is like being a composer who can only write string quartets or something. I mean, if you have never tried to write for full orchestra, how do you know?

What brought about this change?

I wish I knew. I have had a nagging, great, worshipful kind of admiration for figure sculpture all my life. Any sculptor who doesn't find Florence his spiritual home is no sculptor. One simply can't ignore this great pressure from the past. Again and again and again I return to this kind of thing in reading and traveling and just looking at pictures and things in museum collections for some kind of nourishment. Maybe I'm seeking a tuning fork I could always strike to be sure that my instrument is doing what I think it's doing, a way of being sure I was playing in tune.

But again and again as I revisited all these places, the more I traveled, the more I just realized that the greatest stuff I saw was figurative. I toyed with the idea for about a year before I tried it. I began to think that if I didn't try this, I would be much less a bullfighter than I'd like to be, that's all. I was at a good sort of stopping point with my other work it seemed, so I just decided to try it. Oh, I did terrible, discouraging things the first several months because as you can imagine, my taste was far in advance of my abilities. I was ready to shoot myself at the end of the first summer. Terribly discouraging. I must have made forty pieces and destroyed thirty-seven.

Is it going better now?

Oh yes. I've just started to break through now after almost a year. Now I'm at the point where I expect I'll cast some of these things. It's affecting my whole plan for a sabbatical: I didn't know what I was going to do but I *wasn't* going to work. Now I think maybe I'm just going to work. Not here, but somewhere. Europe, Puerto Rico, or somewhere. I just want to work.

If we can agree that the first-rate practicing, involved, producing professional is important to the university in a professional school, what are ways you see the university might be able to elicit a little more commitment from artists?

Well, I don't know too much about artists who complain in any deep and bitter way. Artists, I think, are always discontent. No one would be an artist who didn't want to change things and make things over. I'm trying to think of the kind of discontented person I've met who's an artist. Almost always, he's very young and he's discontented with the university because he's discontented with his life. He would be discontented with the Chase Manhattan Bank if he was working there and hoped to eventually be an officer or something like that. You know, there should be a phrase, "Gloomy as a graduate student" or something. Who isn't, say at about the time of a master's degree, terribly, terribly gloomy? For the first time you've got to face things. The undergraduates are all poets and artists. The graduate students are something else again; there are no answers in the back of the book, you know. You're not repeating somebody else's experiment, you're making up your own experiment. Ph.D. candidates tend finally to get to be a little more cheerful because they have gotten further, they've achieved a little along the way. But I think the general kind of young graduate student artist is just a gloomy, miserable cuss because he's got to work twenty years or more before he can even begin to know how to use his medium and there's no money in it, and it's just a dreadful gamble he's taking, and he lives with that all the time. It's really silly to want to be a high-wire walker, but once you develop a taste for high-wire walking a lot of other things are boring. Well, it's rather silly to want to be a sculptor or poet, but there you are. But you've got to be able to support it, and the discontented people are the people who are keeping a mistress they can't afford. They're afraid they are going to run out of money and ideas before they can achieve anything. It's a very egocentric kind of pursuit—sculpture and painting. After all, you're trying to impose hard, defined images on the world. You're trying to say the world looks the way you say it looks.

A working artist, functioning every day in the studio with great regularity, who is discontented is in the *wrong field*. If you are able to work, you are given enough money to work, a place to work, and you can go in every day and paint or whatever it is, and you're discontented with your life, you shouldn't try to be an artist. I mean it's just a bad experience for some people. Some people shouldn't try to be priests.

What about the guy who says, "I would like very much to have a place to work and enough money to do it and to do it with great regularity, but I don't have time because the university expects me to teach fifteen credit hours," or something like that?

Well, you know, by and large in the ten or fifteen or twenty better universities in the country, people are paid more than a living wage, and one's hourly pay for fifteen contact hours is not bad; as a matter of fact, it's rather impressive. It's a highly paid part-time job. Artists have to have some way of making a living if they aren't rich. I think one should calculate the hourly pay, and if he doesn't like it, go get another job or moonlight or something.

Janos Starker

Janos Starker was born in Budapest July 5, 1924. He was performing at the Franz Liszt Academy (of which he is a graduate) by the time he was eleven. Upon completion of his studies, Starker became first cellist of the Budapest Opera and Philharmonic orchestras.

Starker left Hungary in 1946, traveled in Europe, lived briefly in Paris, and in 1948 settled in the United States, where he was first cellist in the Dallas Symphony Orchestra. He subsequently held similar posts with the Metropolitan Opera and Chicago Symphony orchestras.

Starker is heard annually in most musical capitals of the world. As a recitalist and soloist with orchestras, he tours the United States, Canada, Europe, the Far East, and South America. He records for Angel, Decca, Deutsche Grammophon Gesellschaft, London, Mercury, and Phillips.

Mr. Starker is Distinguished Professor of Music at Indiana University.

Mr. Starker, why did you become a teacher in a university?

In my case, it's simply a dedication to the cause of teaching which dates back to the age of eight, surprisingly enough. That was the first time my teacher assigned a six-year-old to be guided by me. Since that day I have been teaching. It is a matter of trying to divide my life between these two areas—education and performance. For someone like me who plays seventy-five or eighty performances a year and travels around the world, often it is asked, "How is it possible to combine the two, time-wise?"

It is a matter of temperament. I consider myself primarily a pedagogue. I interpret not as a second vocation but as a parallel: it has to be together. If I am not performing, I cannot teach; if I don't teach, then I cannot perform, because both are equally important to me.

Will you explain why you say that if you couldn't perform you couldn't teach?

It means that if somebody is a performing artist by nature then it is obviously just as much a necessity to appear in public as it is to eat and drink or make love. It is something without which we cannot exist. Whether it is performance or simply the production of music, there is this absolute necessity. It's hard to define. I have not had the bad luck of really testing what it means if I do not perform. However, at one time, when I came to America, I did spend ten years with various orchestras, during which time I purposely stopped concertizing and only performed as cellist with orchestras. Eventually it reached the point that I had to go back on stage; whether successfully or unsuccessfully was not even a consideration. I quit orchestra life and decided, "From now on I will perform."

I did not have a job as a teacher. It just accidentally happened that at the time I resigned from my last orchestra post, this university came along and offered me a position which seemed the ideal setup. The past thirteen years have proven it.

You asked why it is necessary since there are so many teachers in the world who are not performing and vice versa. I happen to believe that the reason why there is such a tremendous lack of outstanding violinists in the world is exactly because of that element: the artists of the violin, the best-known artists, do not teach, and that means that the Sterns and the Heifetzes and the Milsteins and the colleagues of that era did not teach. On the other hand, the Russian violinists like Oistrakh and Kogan are teaching, and you see the floods of winners of every international competition from among their students. On the other hand, see what's happening in the cello today. Every single concertizing cellist in the world *is* teaching, the result of which is that we finally have the golden era of cello-playing. We have a mass of cellists all over the world—far more than the market, so to speak, can absorb.

It is essential that the artist teach, because no matter how marvelous a teacher is or how unessential in some sense for the teacher to be able to perform the Tchaikovsky Piano Concerto or the Beethoven Violin Concerto for a student, still the fact that a student enters a room where a respected concert artist already is prepares the ground far better than if the teacher has to spend time to gain respect by explaining and by displaying a great deal of knowledge about the instrument and about music. Obviously it facilitates, speeds up the educational process. If a student who happens to be gifted comes into a studio and cannot hear the teacher quote a phrase at least (not a concerto, but a phrase at least) or demonstrate a sound on the instrument, it is much more difficult for the student to develop properly with this disadvantage.

In some instances it discourages the students if a concert performer gives this demonstration. But those who can be discouraged should not be in the field to begin with. The advantage of it is that it can spur on the talented ones to far greater heights.

I am not interested whether a student comes here to see how well he can prove my pedagogic ability by winning a competition. I am interested that when he goes to another school after he gets his degrees or goes into an orchestra, that he is a fully trained, fully capable musician who can continue alone the education which I started. I am interested in *starting*, not reaping the harvest by winning competitions through my students.

I consider it the same as in ten years of orchestral playing in the United States: I learned more to become what I consider a truly professional musician than by practicing six hours a day in my studio. The same thing, and even more so, is valid as far as teaching is concerned. You learn by teaching what you truly want to do and what you truly attempt to do and what you are capable of doing. If I think back to the age of eight, that I was supposed to explain to a six-year-old how to hold a bow, this forced me finally to find out how one is supposed to hold the bow. I also learned that there are many, many ways of holding the bow and holding the instrument, and making a phrase and everything that pertains to music-making. That is one of the things which is very hard for all the performing musicians to understand: that by teaching, you learn that there are many ways of doing things.

Is it fair for me to say that is a selfish motive?

Everything is selfish. Every charity is selfish. There is no way of separating the two. An example is that if someone in the street is accosted by somebody asking ten cents for a cup of coffee, how many different ways can it be explained if he does give the dime? On one hand, you can say that he is just charitable. You can say that he is selfish because he satisfied his own conscience. You can say he is a cheapskate because he can afford to give a dollar so why does he give only a dime. Everything we do is selfish. To go on stage and perform is selfish. To try to give people as much from your capabilities and musical abilities as you can is awfully selfish.

Selfish reasons are simple. But I (and maybe some others—I can only talk for myself) happen to believe that I am doing something significant in string-playing. Now if somebody is referred to as a trailblazer or attempting new roads in instrumental playing or music-making, obviously it takes time until the public appreciates it. So here comes the selfish reason: by teaching, I spread the understanding of the thing that I am doing on stage.

Do you really enjoy the teaching?

I guess it is quite obvious after this much conversation that I mean it when I say that primarily I am by temperament a pedagogue. That's why I attempt to phrase principles, ideas in such a way that even the child can understand, hopefully. One thing is to speak about the clouds and riddles about what music means, what art means. The other thing is to be able to explain that sounds are created in such and such a way, and if you do this, this is what happens. If you do another thing, what happens then? So I write methods and I write articles about the subject, and so forth.

What about university life bugs you? It's entirely possible for you to be a teacher in a studio in New York, or Berlin, or Paris. You don't have to be a Distinguished Professor of Music at this university to teach. Why are you here?

When you ask what bugs me, naturally my life tends toward the conservatory-type teaching since I am primarily interested in the musical aspect of the thing—not neglecting the academic studies but certainly not at the expense of the musical studies. If it is at the expense of practicing, then I would still prefer that they practice the required number of hours to obtain the skills. Now when this collision occurs, it's inevitable that there are times I am bugged. But it's the same kind of being bugged if you are in any kind of situation where politics enter the picture and others' interests enter the picture. Logically, the theory department is insisting on the significance of the theory teaching and the orchestra director insists on spending a number of hours in the orchestra and this collision of interests is a natural thing.

If I were sitting in the Senate or the Congress, we would fight for roads in this state while somebody else wanted roads in Ohio. All the interests should coincide and they do in many instances, but certain interests are fought for by individuals and that's when we are bugged. But I don't see any dramatic problems. It's not the star teachers who want to be stars. Their positions put them into that seat. There are some people who are disturbed by it, and it is only human that if I concertize all year around and I am not participating, let's say, in as many faculty meetings as the others, those who are forced to do so and are in a situation where they have no choice because they have no reason to go away, obviously they are envious. But these are the petty things which happen in any position, whether it is the Bell Telephone Company or something else. These are not musical problems; these are simply human problems which you are faced with. Either you put up with it with passion or put up with it with understanding. I try to understand everybody else's position and I am grateful that I happen to be in a better position.

When you say that, it doesn't sound as though it is a very big problem for you. You aren't worried about your colleagues, are you?
  I feel compassionate about those colleagues of mine who have problems. I try to do my darndest not to act like a star teacher and not injure them, which means that when I am here, I work three times as much as anybody else because I feel that my career should not be at their expense. It should simply be for the benefit of those who happen to study with me and for my own benefit, but I am trying not to harp on it.

As a practical matter, would you tell me what is your commitment to this school? How are your clock hours arranged? Do you have to teach a certain number of students each semester?
  In our school, I think it is something like nineteen students a major teacher is supposed to take. It depends on the general load of the school. It happens that in the summer session now, in which I am the only cello teacher, thirty-three students have registered. I am here for only a month since my concert obligations take me back to Europe and to Canada and all over the place. Shocking as it is to me at the present time, I am taking care of approximately twenty-seven students, and I give classes, and I start a chamber music seminar with a colleague next week, and I also give a lecture to a teachers' convention here, and then I play a charity concert for a students' emergency fund Wednesday, and so on. And ten days from now, I am on my way to Europe to perform in the Innsbruck Festival and then the Stratford Festival and in Vancouver, and God knows what, and I just came back from playing in Strassburg, Prague, Cardiff, Bremen, Munich, and all sorts of festivals. It is a combination that sounds inconceivable at times, but it is manageable. I still have time to pick my blackberries and to enjoy my friends.

Obviously, if you have stayed for thirteen years, you are not so annoyed with this university or the concept of being a professor that you are about to pull up stakes and leave. When I asked you about annoyances, there seemed to be no fundamental problems in respect to your connection with this university.

I don't have any fundamental problems. I always say that if another school offered me more money to teach less with the same amount of liberty, then of course I would pull up stakes. I'm not totally dedicated or chauvinistic about our place. I want the opportunity to teach the way I want, which means the kind of students I want. The reason I am here is that it is giving me the maximum in that.

We can delve into other problems or other situations. Obviously you must have gotten some other answers. The very fact of college-town existence can produce a great deal of strain in some people. They feel they are closed in, far away from big cities or so-called big cultural centers. I feel that our place is a cultural center in itself. For me, getting off the plane coming from Paris or Amsterdam or from whatever big city and after a forty-five-minute drive finding myself in my house where cows still walk around our fence is absolutely beautiful. It's simply gorgeous and I can still breathe the air and I can pick my beautiful roses. For me this is absolutely ideal, and I would hate the thought that for some fantastic-sounding offer I would even contemplate going to live in a big city to teach in a conservatory. Then again, this may be a problem for an awful lot of teachers. For me this is ideal and beautiful. I can hardly wait to get off the plane and get back to little Camelot.

Let's talk some more about an ideal situation.

The same with fewer students.

In so many ways, this seems an ideal situation.

That it is. Otherwise I wouldn't be here. As I said, I don't need it; I have it by choice. I am giving seminars and classes all over the world. If I give seminars for a week, I make more money than in two months in the university this summer, so I don't need it. But that doesn't provide me with the possibility of really raising a generation of musicians in the way I believe they should be raised. For me, it's a dedication to a cause and this provides me with the opportunity.

I'm sorry that I cannot sound really disgusted about the situation but I am sure that an awful lot of people are using this opportunity to sound off and say all. I can tell you all the bad things about the university but it doesn't really involve me.

You can tell me?

Oh, I can tell you a lot of things.

Let's hear some of the bad things.

For instance, the teacher who doesn't concertize much hates the guts of those who do, and he doesn't have the same position with the university administration. They do not travel as much and they have more of the duties here. The other teachers who are not in the position that a handful of us here are in have all the headaches: they have to teach too much, they have to participate in too many faculty meetings, they have to make too many faculty decisions, there are too many auditions, too many tapes to be listened to, and they are bored to death with it obviously. These all exist; it's all here. You know well. I am not needed to tell you about university problems with the policy-deciding process and so on. But since I am the one who interferes with policy decisions, I can't complain. If I am not here, I don't have to participate. Those things are difficult but they don't touch me.

In Europe, when we studied in the conservatory we had at least two lessons a week. There is one in the university, so if you conceive of a man who is working toward a bachelor's degree, four years, let's contemplate the eight semesters of work. During this eight semesters he gets twenty-eight lessons a year. It's far from enough in order to really learn the skill of music-making—learn that trade (let's use that word). That's one of the reasons, for instance, that I invented in this school the piano chamber music class. I did it on my own. I don't insist that people enroll in it for credit. They just participate and listen and then some of those who get it for credit get a grade—if I remember who they are, and some of them are just simply sitting in the class. The educational process, as far as I'm concerned, is not based on credit systems. On the other hand, you cannot do away with it because you still have to find the means and ways of ruling that somebody has accomplished a certain amount that is necessary for a standard bachelor's degree or a master's degree or a doctor's degree. As far as I'm concerned, a doctor's degree in instrumental playing is total nonsense.

I don't want to press this point forever, but I want to ask one more question: if I came to this institution and I were gifted and had reasonable facility and had come specifically to study with you, would you teach me? What if at our first meeting I said, "I have absolutely no aspiration to be a concert artist; I want to be a teacher," would you take me as a student?

Well, there are a number of them here. You don't have to *say* it, because when you sit down and play ten notes, it's obvious that you are not going to be a concert artist. Now in ten notes it's not going to come out that you are a teacher; the ten notes shows it negative for the artist's career. But if the person has the basic ability and digital ability and mental ability (which also comes out in the first conversation), then I teach the student. Unless it is at the expense of somebody else who has a better chance of developing faster. Then I feel that I can give more attention to that one.

On the other hand, I give classes and everybody is entitled or required to attend those classes—even those who are not my students, to be sure they still get the benefit of my presence here. That's what the chamber music class is for; that's what the seminars are for. My seminar is not only for my students; all string players come.

There is a matter of curriculum which I've pressed through in this institution which is not even known. A student is allowed to take any course with any teacher. In many instances I have bassoon players, flute players, viola players who study with me if I happen to have room. The idea should be that in a school like ours or like yours where there are a number of outstanding teachers, the student should not be imprisoned by one teacher's studio but he should have the benefit of all the others. Only those teachers object to that who believe they are the only ones who can spread knowledge and the only way of making music is their way. I happen to believe there are many ways of making music, and if anybody wants to become a professional he is supposed to learn many ways and all ways. Therefore I admit a lot of students to come try to benefit from what I can give, and I send my students to listen to all the others as well.

Help me understand this thing you've initiated here. When the bassoonist and the percussionist and the trumpet player and the pianist come to your classes, they don't actually play the instruments, do they? They just observe your lessons and. . . .

No. In many instances they come and play for me and wait for instruction on their instruments because. . . .

On their instruments. Good grief!

And it's not how to put their finger on the bassoon but simply how to play phrases and how to make music and possibly how to help by application of certain physical principles which are identical for all instruments: how to improve their playing.

That's very interesting. Is it very widely taken?

No. We don't like to make it very wide because it's only those exceptionally gifted or intelligent students who realize that while admiring their own teacher, still they feel that there are other fields to learn and they come around. I am not the only one. There are a number of teachers who are in this position. We don't like to popularize it because this is one of the things which at times might make other colleagues jealous, since they feel that it may reflect badly upon them that their student goes to a colleague who doesn't even know how to play the flute and studies with him. This is, of course, a general political problem and it exists anywhere in the world, not just in the colleges.

In a hypothetical situation, if you were to become dean of this school tomorrow, what are some of the first things you would do in terms of change and development?

Well, most likely I would attempt the impossible: to reduce the number of students and reduce the number of teachers and try to weed out those who are not fully functioning in the school for its benefit and for the students'. But as you know, we have the tenure system, and whether I am the dean or he is the dean, neither can do it. We cannot fight it. I have fought for many years in my professional musical existence against this so-called security that we all humanly need and we humanly desire for everybody. On the other hand, it is a horrifying problem that many of the people who happen to function in the musical world are partially skilled laborers ultimately and not truly artists, and that element is annoying to the artist-teacher, as well as to anybody in any field where you find people who are not truly qualified to participate in the teaching process or political process or whatnot. They are still there and you cannot eliminate them. Humanly you cannot do it, but on the other hand, under the artistic conscience, I wish I were in a position where I could eliminate, let's say, 20 to 30 percent of the faculty and students. That would set things on a higher standard. It is a collision of artistic intentions and human sympathy.

Is there anything else you would do if you were the dean besides reduce the school's population?

As a string player, of course I would upgrade chamber music, because chamber music is the single most neglected aspect in music schools—the significance in crediting it, significance in assigning top-notch teachers for it, and significance in hour distribution of how much time should be spent with it.

This is not a local problem or a school problem; this is an international problem. The great music appreciation that we all cry after which existed in Germany up until World War II was due to the fact that the people themselves made music. When we contemplate the thousands and thousands of students studying music, we know that a large percentage of them do not pursue musical careers. They will do something else. But in the meantime, if they are properly trained, they will keep music as a daily necessity all their lives. If they are not trained to make chamber music, they will forget their musical training easier. With chamber music they can pursue the music, at least at home or in small circles, and therefore the genuine music appreciation is taken care of. I talk haltingly now because it is a huge problem which cannot be isolated to the schools. It is something which I fully believe in personally: that the secret of music appreciation in any given country is how many people there make music, and chamber music is the quickest way to do it, or choral singing. These two aspects are not sufficiently taken care of, which means that the students in music schools are not required to spend enough time in singing and in chamber music.

It is our problem to devise a curriculum which provides the proper amount of time to be spent on it. But if I were the dean in this school, beyond what I said (weeding out the lower quality), I would upgrade choral singing and chamber music teaching.

That reminds me of Kodály. A man told me yesterday that if he were the dean, the first thing he would do is abandon the requirement here that all students sing in the chorus for four years. He couldn't see very much use in it—and I'm putting it mildly! You, on the other hand, are saying that it's a positive aesthetic force, absolutely fundamental to music-making.

It is fundamental because no musician will ever successfully exist who is unable to sing a phrase, and this is one of the tragic things in our music education. Students come here, horrifying problems are detected, and ultimately it comes out that they are unable to sing a phrase. The question of balance as to how far this choral singing should go is up for negotiation. How far chamber music playing should go is too. But they prevent students learning one line all their lives and thinking that's the only line important to music. That goes into artistic problems. I don't want to make a wide statement, but an awful lot of those colleagues who make this sort of sick statement are, in my estimation, responsible for a lot of ills in the musical world. I simply feel sorry for those who have not realized what are the essential things in music-making. They think that if the student practices eight hours a day in a studio and learns a piece, he can win a competition. If that's the solution to the educational problem, then it's not for me.

I'm still a full believer in professionalism, which means that a professional should be able to sing and should be able to play his instrument and should be able to play jazz or symphony or opera and whatnot.

By your life's example and from the things you've said to me, I know you think it's important that a concert artist, no matter how renowned he is and no matter how pressing his world engagements, ought to teach. I believe that too, and that's why I'm here. What, then, are the ways universities could elicit from people exactly like you the kind of commitment that you have to this institution and to teaching? What kinds of things could make other artists like you want to join a faculty?

You cannot elicit responsibility. You can provide the grounds. You can invite somebody to come and teach. You tell him that here is the situation. If possible, ask him to teach only twelve students. If school resources cannot be found for limiting the number to that, then it is the artist's responsibility to determine if he is willing to take more. Give him the leeway to fulfull his obligations on the concert stage and see whether he can fit into the picture, because not everybody can fit into it.

There are some people who will do it for temporary relief from insecurity of bookings or something of that sort and it will turn up very quickly. An awful lot of people came here and they just couldn't fill the post. They couldn't mix. They couldn't get into the whole situation. You only hope you will find somebody who will find satisfaction and find room if he happens to have a dedication to the cause. And he either does or he doesn't.

The important thing is never to engage an artist-teacher with tenure. And only engage him with the understanding that either he fulfills the requirements of what the university wants and that he himself finds satisfaction, or somebody else has to be there. Not everybody is capable of doing this double existence, or triple existence, or whatever. It's administration as well as education, it's concertizing as well as recording for most of us, and some of us are writing. Some people will not be able to do it. Some will have wives and families who cannot fit into this thing. It's a gamble in every instance. It should not be a final, irrevocable kind of decision.

Do I understand you to say it boils down to a human problem?

Yes. Some people are teachers and some are not. When I said I would cut 20 or 30 percent, it is not necessarily because these people are not good; they just don't fit into the picture, either humanly or instrumentally, or they are simply not teachers.

You will think me very stupid, but I simply don't understand exactly what you mean by "don't fit into the picture."

Let's say somebody is concertizing and one day is on stage with the idolatry, the cheers, and the standing ovations. The next day, he comes back and sits at ten o'clock in the studio with a student who may not quite be ready for that lesson. He has to show him fingerings and bowings and speak about how to hold the bow. He may be just unable to synchronize these things. As a minor example, he may be unable to bear the fact that from the Savoy Hotel in London he is back here. Let's say that concert life is as glamorous as it can be. In spite of all the problems of traveling, it is a very glamorous existence if you are successful. Here the school does not provide glamor. It is not supposed to. It is supposed to simply provide ground where, if you are dedicated to the teaching, then you are able to teach. An artist who is one day playing with the world's most famous conductor, the next day arrives back here, and suddenly you hear that the school orchestra is having trouble because the cello section is not good enough. You have to deal with that. And you say, "Oh well, it's not my problem." It *is* your problem. If it is not your problem, then go someplace else. Then you are not supposed to be in the university.

But you are a man who can synchronize these things.

Well, so far I am still healthy. I have no heart attacks behind me and no ulcers and that's why I have done it. But maybe two years hence I will have these problems. I don't know. Thank God, I haven't had any yet.

John Wustman

John Wustman was born in Byron Center, Michigan. He studied
at the University of Michigan (B.Mus.) and with Leonard Shure
in New York. He has held Fulbright and two American Specialists grants to South America.

Mr. Wustman is heard in frequent performances and recordings as pianist with Elisabeth Schwarzkopf, Birgit Nilsson,
Regine Crespin, Roberta Peters, Cesare Siepi, Nicolai Gedda,
and other internationally active singers.

Mr. Wustman teaches at the University of Illinois.

*Mr. Wustman, not many big careers have been made in accompany-
ing. Would you prefer a term such as "vocal chamber music?"*

I just call it *music*. I don't think it needs any further explana-
tion. If one wants to call it "accompanying" it doesn't bother
me; it's a perfectly fine term. I don't think it really matters
whether you are playing the piano while someone is singing, or
someone is playing the violin, or the cello, or a whole string
quartet is playing, or if you are playing all by yourself. The
basic problem is that one still has to play the piano. And one
has to do it well.

I can't tell you how many times I have had letters from students around the country, or phone calls, while I was still living
in New York and now that I'm teaching here, saying, "I would
love to come study with you. I want to be an accompanist because I don't think I'm good enough to be a pianist." That very
often is the way that I'm approached and my answer always is,
"Well, if you're not good enough to be a pianist, then you're
certainly not good enough to be an accompanist, so I think we'd
better forget the whole business."

*Why don't you ask them what instrument it is they intend playing
when they accompany?*

It's hardly their fault; it's that they hear so much that isn't really very good. One hears so many people, especially those who play for singers, who really don't play very well. They just sort of make a stab at everything and their primary goal is that they should not be too loud and that they shouldn't be any faster or any slower than the singer. That's all.

And I must say to the discredit of most singers, whether they be students, semi-professionals, or professionals, that many seem to have the same feeling about an accompanist. There are several outstanding exceptions; there is no doubt about that. But I think very often that a singer is very happy with anybody who plays the piano if it seems that he plays most of the right notes, is not too loud, not too fast or too slow for what they intend to do. But I find very often, especially with professionals, that they have no real idea what the music itself is about. They cannot view a song or an aria as a piece of music but only as a vehicle to display their glorious organ.

A vehicle for "the instrument."

Right. Or *"the voice,"* as they always call it: "The voice isn't so good today." And I always say, "The voice: does that mean yours or mine?" Why can't people say, "My voice just doesn't feel very good today?" The voice: it's as if it's something *outside* of you. This, of course, is the biggest problem that singers face. "The voice" exists *inside* them. It makes much more sense for me to say, "The piano isn't in tune very well." It's *outside* of me, so it can be "the piano."

Well, let's get to the point of the matter. I'm curious to know how you were attracted to the University of Illinois to teach. What kind of influences and factors were at work in your own life but also in the world at large to make you decide to come here?

I hadn't thought about teaching here or any other place at all. It just so happened that one day in August, several years ago, the dean called me and told me Mr. Ulanowsky had died (which I knew) and asked if I were interested. I thought for two minutes and said yes, I was interested and that I would let him know the next day.

I think, just to be absolutely honest about it, the biggest at-
traction was the money, and the security of it. I doubt if very
many people make an absolutely smashing living at playing
concerts. They can make very nice livings, better than average;
probably somewhat like mine. But not anywhere secure at all.

My own is especially precarious because it's so dependent
upon someone else. Recently I was going to have a big tour
with Schwarzkopf with eleven or twelve concerts and she sang
the first two, and then (something wrong with her throat) she
called me and said, "I'm sorry, but I'm going to cancel all the
rest. I'm going home to Switzerland." Well, there I was. I was
unhappy because I like her so much and I was looking forward
to playing. But my world didn't fall apart. I still had my teaching, and my salary, and could pay the mortgage, and eat, and
wasn't frantic.

But several years ago, that would have meant—let's see: she
canceled ten concerts; that took almost all of March for me, during which time I had not accepted anything else, and this happened the last day of February. Where was I going to find ten
concerts immediately to replace those ten I lost?

*I think anyone who is even remotely aware knows what the eco-
nomic situation in the arts is now. Obviously it's perfectly comfortable for a person such as you to discuss this candidly, because anyone can open the* New York Times *Sunday edition to the music
section and find, with frequency and regularity, the caption "John
Wustman at the Steinway." But it's not very shocking news for anyone to know that it's a precarious life, even for the most active and
visible people involved.*

And the recital field is simply disappearing, except for the
most famous people. I recently used to play at least ninety-five
to a hundred concerts every season, from October to May. Now
it has come to be forty or forty-five, through no overt action of
mine: I haven't said, "I'm sorry, I don't want to play anymore."
It's just that they simply don't exist. That's all. I would happily
play a hundred again.

Would you really?

Well, not now I guess. I like it too much at the university. And time off for a hundred I would never get. I mean I wouldn't be here at all. When I found out I would come here, I looked through my schedule and said, "Oh yes, I can come these days, and those days, and here I have two weeks free, and here are ten days, and whatnot." (I was looking at my concert book when I did that.) And then when I got here, I realized that all of those periods of time I had were holidays. It was Christmas when I had two weeks and it was Easter when I had ten days, and of course there was no school.

Was there anything else except the security involved in drawing you to this university to teach?

Yes, one other big thing: this university was the only one in the country, as far as I knew, that had a tradition of having someone like me on the faculty. I knew that they had George Reeves in the late 1950s and then Mr. Ulanowsky from, I think, 1960 until 1968. And I knew that they were used to coping with the fact that I would be gone a great deal, and that it would be very irregular, and whatnot. The situation here is set up extremely well—in fact, it's ideal. I don't know if there's any other job quite like it. I have quite a few students; I can't even tell you how many because I've never counted them. But the students I have do not get credit for studying with me. This is absolutely extracurricular, which means that also I do not have to give them a grade. It saves me all that monkey business. It saves me from any kind of responsibility of having to make up lessons that are missed. There is nothing in the catalog or in any university school of music bylaw which says that someone is entitled to twenty-four lessons with me.

The singing teachers here have a load to maintain. They are contracted to teach so many hours per week for which the students get credit. A half-hour, or—I don't understand the credit system, but say he gets one unit for that, and for one unit he is supposed to get thirty lessons. (I'm making up the numbers.)

So, if the teacher goes away and doesn't make them up, the student has a really legitimate complaint. He can go to the office and say, "I paid my tuition. I'm supposed to have thirty lessons, and so-and-so has only given me twenty-two. I think this is unfair." And the student is right, if it is promised to him in that fashion. But with me, it isn't so. That also appealed to me enormously.

Did you have some sort of qualms about university teaching?

Yes! I thought that it might be too confining, that I might be held down, that somebody would say, "Yes, you must give fifteen hours a week," or something like that. I still don't think I could have given fifteen hours a week in the beginning.

How many hours a week do you teach, on the average? I realize you can't give me a precise figure.

I haven't the faintest idea. But during the summer session, the average is about thirty or thirty-one.

You make up in the summer what you don't do in the winter?

Yes. I feel some moral responsibility, after all. And I see no other way to get the work done. You see, I play for all my students who give recitals here.

How does one become a student of yours? If I attend the University of Illinois and I'm a singer, do I merely walk into your studio and say, "Mr. Wustman, I'm a singer and I would like you to coach me?"

Well, I would listen to you first.

You have the power then to reject anyone with whom you don't feel it's a reasonable association?

It's not quite that good. I wish it were. The school has a tradition (again, it's a tradition—there is nothing written in a catalog or any such thing) that all senior voice majors and all graduate voice majors are entitled to what they like to term "coaching." And there is another coach on the staff also. So they all are supposedly entitled to some. And they have something worked out that if they are not giving a recital during a semester they should have half an hour a week; if they are giving a recital, then they are entitled to one hour a week.

I find that half-hours are totally useless so I don't teach any half-hours at all. Because I'm away a lot, I can't schedule someone to come at eleven o'clock on Tuesday morning throughout the year. Maybe I'll be gone ten Tuesdays—I really don't know. So usually in the fall, I start them all out with an hour a week. Then as the spring comes, and their recitals draw near, I take them every day for at least an hour, and sometimes for an hour and a half. But as soon as they give their recitals, then I drop them and concentrate on the others. Last spring, in April or May, I played sixteen recitals here.

That sounds to me like a remarkably practical as well as almost ideal situation for everybody involved—the student, principally.

I think it is too. And it's the only thing that really makes sense.

If you had several years, perhaps you could really build up something by going one hour a week, and slowly, slowly the wall would get built up, you know, a little brick here and a little brick there. But when it comes time to do a performance, the most helpful thing is this really intensive work, say two weeks before, every day.

I think most of my students have done quite remarkable recitals here. It varies, of course, with their own ability. I mean you can't make a Fischer-Dieskau out of everybody. You can try; but you really can't. But something really does happen with this everyday working.

Tell me, then: you have not had a very long affiliation with a university, but from what experience you've had, what has been satisfying and rewarding to you?

The same things I've been telling you, really. I like the freedom. I don't have to be in at nine in the morning. I can start when I feel like it. I don't have to stop at four; I can stop at six. I can teach all day Saturday, which I very often do. I was here this year during the spring vacation. I have a very special liking and affinity for the songs of Hugo Wolf and I have made this a big specialty. This past year, I did all of the *Möricke Lieder*—all fifty-three—we did them in two evenings. The time was a little short because the kids were involved in opera, and I had been away, and I happened to have Easter week free. So I told them I would come here three days and that we would have Wolf classes nine hours a day—ten to one, two to five, and seven to ten. So they all stayed during spring vacation. It was marvelous. The school was empty. At night there wasn't a light on in the place. It was just great. It was very concentrated work, and very rewarding.

Do you like to teach?
I love teaching.

Why?
I suppose because I'm very good at it. It satisfies my ego. And I like to see people develop. I like to see them grow. But I think you have to be good at it to like it. I honestly do.

We're really not talking about a few years because you've been coaching some of the world's greatest singers for a long career.
Yes, for a long time in New York. This is the first university teaching with a regular salary. When I used to teach in New York, if somebody called up and said, "I can't come today because I have an audition," or "I didn't sleep well," or "I got my period this morning," that means I also didn't get paid. Here it doesn't matter: they can have abortions and babies and God only knows what, but I get paid anyway. It doesn't matter.

I don't mean to sound crass about the money part, but I think you do have to be damn good at teaching to be able to enjoy it. I know teachers who just hate teaching; they really are doing it because they can't do anything else. Somehow, one has to put in considerably less hours to make a rather comfortable salary teaching than one would have to put in in an office job.

What do you think is wrong in the lives of these people who are terribly unhappy as teachers? What's the difference between you and them?

They are bitter and they are frustrated.

Why? Because they're trying to teach people to do something they never actually did or perhaps never could do themselves—is that the answer?

Yes. I think you're right on both counts. One could say it still another way. It's something that they really would like to do, but don't have the courage to admit that they don't "have it" to do it with.

You say you like to teach. Are there students whom you don't like to teach, or students who are not very rewarding for you, and if so, what kind of people are they?

Almost none. There have been a couple. But I find that by and large I actually love them all—with one or two exceptions. I am terribly enthusiastic about it, and I'm very enthusiastic about certain aspects of the repertory—not all of it. This is purely subjective; there are some parts of the repertory that I don't really much care for—I don't enjoy teaching it, I don't really enjoy playing it—but there are big hunks of it that I really do adore, and I think students are very, very quick to respond to that kind of enthusiasm, which I think they see all too rarely. They are very eager; they work very hard; and they try very hard. Often marvelous things happen to people that you think were nothing—that nothing would ever happen to. I can sometimes see them transformed inside of an hour.

I used to have a colleague who said, "You can't make a silk purse out of a sow's ear." You're not convinced of that, it seems to me.

No, I'm not convinced of that, but basically, it really is true I guess. As I said to you earlier, you can't make a Fischer-Dieskau or Schwarzkopf out of everybody.

But as a professor in this institution must you have Fischer-Dieskau to be working with?

Absolutely not. I think preferably not.

Why "preferably"?
I'd have nothing to teach them.

Let me ask you another question then—a fairly delicate one, I suppose: it regards your relationship with your colleagues. What you do here is take a singer's students and teach them how to make music. Is that fairly accurate so far?
Let's put it a little bit differently. I take a singing teacher's students and try to teach them how to sing music.

I thought that was what I'd said. Maybe you're being diplomatic.
I think mine is a bit clearer. You see, I don't think that these things are so terribly, terribly separate. I remember when I was first going to teach in South America. There were newspaper interviews and whatnot, and somebody would introduce me and say that I was there to teach "interpretation." Well, I really don't know what that is.

You're there to teach music, aren't you?
Yes. *Only.* They said I was there to teach "style." I don't know what that is either. It's all something that comes out of the music, and you have to understand an awful lot about the music. You have to understand the languages very well because we deal constantly with *words;* the words make most of the expression. The music helps, but the words also help the music. If the words are useless or unintelligible, then we might just as well hear the same song played on the cello; it might even be better. But you have to understand something about the singing mechanism. I have nothing to do with what is called "technique"—like where to put your tongue, put your jaw here, and lower your eyeballs this way—I have nothing to do with all that monkey business.

Have you ever seen a conductor who really knows nothing about singing (maybe even a great conductor) try to coach soloists in an oratorio performance, say? It's very funny. It's ludicrous because he doesn't really know how to extract something out of this creature that we call a singer. They need very special understanding. They are special animals. They are marvelous ones, wonderful ones. But you have to understand how to get it out. It doesn't go the same as with a violinist.

So far, we've talked about students, and we've talked a little about your colleagues. Let me ask you another question or two about colleagues. I'm curious whether you would go to Walla Walla, Washington, to teach where there was not one other performing musician.

No. I think that would be very difficult, and I don't think I would unless forced to for economic reasons. I certainly wouldn't want to do it.

You need your colleagues as a kind of . . . what?

Yes, what? That's a damn good question. I don't know if I need them at all. I think it's important to have some other people around you who understand something about performance, whether they have done it on a very small scale (like one faculty recital per year) or they have played a Mozart concerto with the Peoria Symphony, or sung the *Messiah* someplace a few times. They have *some* feeling. But that really is not performing in the same sense as performing constantly in all the big cities where (my phrase for it is) your head is really on the block.

Now there is a great tendency in the country to denigrate the importance of New York; I think that's all silly. New York *is* the musical capital of the country, and perhaps the whole world. It's quite one thing to play there and another thing to play in Walla Walla, Washington. And in New York, and Washington, and Chicago, and San Francisco, and Dallas, your head is really on the block. There are critics who are read (whether one thinks they are good critics or not is beside the point). But they come and they review, and you are heard probably by a more discerning group of people. If you play in New York, and Carnegie Hall seats 2,700 or 2,800 people out of a city of 8 million, you can be damn sure that those 2,800 really know what's going on. They're not just coming to while away the time. They come because they hope and think that you are going to uplift them, and they know what to expect. I think your head is really on the block from the standpoint of the newspapers, and also the standpoint of serving the music: it has to be awfully good. It's been difficult at this university for some people to accept that in me. I have my own way of preparing for every concert that I play here. I treat it all just like Carnegie Hall; to me, it's just as important, because the music is as important. Some people don't see why on the day I play concerts that I don't teach six hours too. I have very good reasons why I don't: there's only so much creative energy one can put out. Even if you're superhuman, there's just so much that one mortal can put out in one twenty-four-hour time span, and if you give it all to teaching hard six or seven hours, there's precious little left for the evening to also perform. It's just stupid—you can only do so much.

Well, that brings up another question that I'm very interested in: what do you think has happened to your own professional life as a result of university affiliation? What I'm asking is not a factual question about it; how do you feel *about what may have happened to it?*

I think it has only enriched it. Whenever you teach anything, you learn a great deal. There is no doubt about that. There are certain songs that I have played maybe hundreds of times. Now that I am teaching, when you have to really explain to someone who has come from a little town someplace, a farm someplace, hasn't even heard of Hugo Wolf, you have to begin explaining in detail what this is all about. You find that you learn so damn much about it, and that's the enriching part of it.

That whole Wolf repertory I have played for Schwarzkopf over and over; we've given lots of all-Wolf concerts in various parts of the world. I always thought that I understood it extremely well, I thought I played it well, and now that I'm teaching it I see how much I really didn't know about it. If I could do all those concerts over again now I think they'd be better. They would be twice as good.

Everything you take into yourself makes you richer and

makes you able, I think, to give out more. I think, for instance, that I have played much better in these last half-dozen years than I did before, and I don't think it's just being older, and life; I really think this constant exposure to teaching and young students forces you to think more, forces you to feel more deeply all the things that you believed in the first place and *knew* were true, but this only reinforces it.

Intuitively felt, believed, and knew, but had never been forced to confirm by any kind of outside "checking"?

Right. And you are forced because you have to convince, and you cannot convince someone else of something unless you are convinced.

Sometimes, you know, you get students who are terribly, terribly bright; very gifted either vocally and intellectually or sometimes only intellectually. And sometimes they see things that I have never seen before or have simply taken for granted. They ask "Why this?" and "Why that?" and they are demanding an answer. It forces you to put all of your gray cells into motion.

Because I'm so involved in teaching songs and almost exclusively with the German repertory I do a great deal of teaching of language and poetry and all that has to do with the Romantic movement in German art and whatnot. Every year or so there are two or three students who are either linguistically gifted or really know a lot; they want to know *why*. Why this particular tense? Why this symbolic reference to this, that, and the other? They must have an answer and sometimes I know already because somebody asked me that before; but very often I just say, "I don't know; I just always believed that, and I don't know why," and it forces me to figure out why. Then that becomes a part of you and builds another brick in the building of you as a person.

You haven't said much about administration. There are some persons who make a regular practice of going around complaining about administrators.

I think it's quite difficult to be an administrator. You have to understand a great deal about many different kinds of people. I have my own needs which (for me to be happy here or any other place I might teach) have to be satisfied. If I'm going to be paid a lot of money, my needs must be satisfied in order for me to be able to give my best; otherwise, part of the salary is just wasted. That's what administrators really have to realize, I think. It's not enough just to say, "I'll hire William Primrose—period. Pay him what he wants, or whatever I can afford—period." Well, if you stick him in a room he doesn't like and can't play in and can't teach in and that makes him unhappy, you're getting nothing out of him except his name in the catalog, right?

You're not going to gripe very much, are you?
I would if I had something to gripe about.

Suppose I were here as a representative of another institution trying to hire you. Tell me what kinds of properties of another institution might be able to attract you to it.
I've had three other big offers this year. The important one that nobody seems to come up with as much as Illinois is the amount of *freedom*.

By "freedom" you mean the time to pursue a professional career, is that right?
Yes. Ideally, what I would like to happen is that in such a place I could work with the most gifted singers in the school and those pianists who would like to become accompanists; that I could supervise all that they do and that all their recitals would be supervised by me. That, I think, would be ideal from my standpoint.

I think again it comes down to this question of being free. To be free to teach as you want but also to be free to come and go as you need to come and go. My going away from here and playing at other places and for other singers sort of recharges my batteries again, and I come back all raring to go.

I see the ones who never go away. By the end of the school year, forget it! I think they're just putting in their time, that's all. Not all, but some; they're so bored with it and so tired, and "Oh, thank God it's Friday; thank God so-and-so is going to graduate," etc. Well, I just never feel like that—just never. It's good to have this ability to go away and have other experiences. You come back and have something more to give. But if you only just give and give, pretty soon you are out.

But what we're talking about is not "freedom"; what we're talking about is time. *The scientist can be very free in a university, and the linguist can be very free in a university without going away. But the musician to be free (in the sense that you're using the term) has to have time to go to London and other places.*

Right. And he has to be trusted, knowing if he has to go to London, that he's going not only to enrich himself for his own sake, but to enrich himself so that he then gives more to the university.

Toward a Richer Academic Life

The interviews touched sensitive nerves and provoked discussions on many topics. From these, what lessons can be learned that will benefit all—artist-professors, traditional academics, students, the university, society?

This essay explores these questions by inquiring about the nature of the work liberal arts and fine arts professors engage in. Three dimensions of faculty life—teaching, creative activity, and the environment in which work is carried out—are selected for intensive inquiry. The analysis proceeds by examining what creative artists and academic scholars have in common, what is unique to each, and then assays what each can contribute to the other to improve the quality of university and creative life.

The essay concludes by weighing the contributions each constituency can make. We find that both traditional academics and artists could benefit if they would but observe the other. Even then, artists will give more than they receive, and the long-time residents in the university will profit by heeding how the new settlers conduct their professional lives.

TEACHING

Despite visible surface contrasts as pedagogues, painters and physicists have more instructional practices, attitudes, and goals in common than either believes is the case. For example, professors in both the fine and liberal arts most often teach as they were taught—modeling their style after the best teacher they ever had, after, of course, having mended his minor flaws. If they have assumed a new style, it is one which emerged from having experimented with novel techniques conducted on a trial-and-error basis. Neither collects evidence of the pedagogical results but rather accepts or rejects what he does on the basis of impressions from non-random responses. While both faculty groups admire expertise and respect demonstrated truths, neither sociologists nor sculptors read what is known about teaching, nor does either turn to the university's resources on instruction.

In addition to valuing good teaching, political scientists and poets believe they are far better at it than the typical pedagogue. (In fact, they might say they were "quite extraordinary" if not restrained by modesty.) They worry about their teaching, work hard at it, and wish to improve as teachers. Both believe person-to-person instruction is the essence of genuine teaching. Forced to make curricular decisions between professional and liberal courses for their students, both believe that specialization outweighs the virtues of a broad or liberal education even though they admire the Renaissance Man. Moreover, both believe that one's special expertise is *the* essential ingredient for the successful college teacher.[1]

The artist and liberal arts professor desire the same goal as the consequent of their teaching: a highly knowledgeable, skilled, and creative individual. Cellist and chemist may debate *means* from time to time (how better to finger a chord or remove an impurity from a sample), but their *ends* vary hardly at all. Therefore, on typical ingredients of teaching, neither group has much to contribute to the other, although both could learn from experts in the teaching field. However, the unique pedagogical characteristics of each lay the groundwork for what the indigenous faculty have to offer the homesteaders and what, in turn, the natives might learn from the recent arrivals.

For example, the artist finds the university's instructional paraphernalia particularly bothersome. Credits, grades, time schedules, and the like interfere with instruction, as artists perceive it. In the same (and hence paradoxical) breath the artist advocates the university's certification process, the legitimizing of his student with the awarding of the graduate degree, even

1. It needs to be pointed out that these shared attitudes regarding fundamentals of instruction are unsubstantiated myths most faculty hold. While they may be true, no evidence exists to support them.

though he knows the holder of a degree is not a proven artist and that a degree cannot serve as a sufficient credential for a university position.

A second paradox the artist-professor wrestles with that his counterpart across campus has already either resolved or suppressed stems from an inner compulsion: the artist feels a professional call. He must teach so as to pass on what he has been privileged to acquire. At the same time, he strongly doubts that what he feels obligated to teach can in fact really be taught by anyone. Since the artist-professor's insight rests heavily on non-verbalized knowledge, he has deep reservations about the very essence of instruction. The anatomy professor does not suffer these same self-doubts.

As a corollary to the non-traditional symbolization of his expertise, the artist believes he must continue as a producing artist; that he is a practicing artist is his principal teaching strength. Some liberal arts professors endorse this "demonstrator" role model of the pedagogue. More do not, however, and most do not practice it. Their research or scholarship most often is pursued without any apparent connection to their instruction and is not visible except to a few doctoral students.

These differences in instructional practice lead to considerations of what the classical pedagogues can learn from the fine artists, and vice versa. The natives have two features which the new residents might note and adapt to their particular circumstance. One feature concerns a practice; the other dimension involves a shade of difference with respect to a goal. Both differences can be witnessed best by focusing on a final product of the formal educational process, the advanced graduate.

Mainline academics practice sponsorship, the placing of their students with academic appointments in colleges and universities. Furthermore, the student's dissertation frequently involves the major professor's research area. Hence joint publishing by novice and veteran result and can continue after graduation, especially through the critical early steps of the novitiate's scholarly career. Nothing predicts future productivity as accurately as early productivity. The earlier a person publishes, the more he will publish over his lifetime. Continued assistance beyond the formal university certification procedures has much to do with the budding scholar's long-time contribution. It may be the critical period in deciding whether he will become a productive scholar or, like altogether too many of equal promise, only a rare and/or occasional contributor.

The arts differ, of course. The individuality of the enterprise militates against cooperative ventures. At the same time, the interviews suggest that a complete severing between teacher and student does little good. Indeed, the artist has to make it on the merit of his own work. So does the successful scholar. But throwing the bird out of the nest doesn't make better Jonathan Livingston Seagulls. Continued association does. Artist-teachers could better realize the fulfillment of their purposes by devising ways to maintain collegial relationships with their professional offspring. Some of the established academic practices can guide artists.

Finally, traditional faculty would profit immensely from a visit to artists' studios. There the professor at work is on public display and some secrets of the creative process are revealed. The student can observe work in progress—mistakes as well as ingenious solutions.

How does the budding historian or philosopher learn to do history or to philosophize? His professor remains invisible, except perhaps through the window in his carrel in the graduate library or through a glimpse of his study at a tea in his home. At unpredictable and irregular times, the academic professor emerges with the finished product, the final draft of the manuscript, like an Athena emerging from the head of Zeus.

What prompted the inquiry? How many false starts were made? How and when did the breakthrough and key insight take place? These and related critical ingredients of the creative process remain invisible. We know Newton did not begin his inquiry with his eight definitions and three axioms and then systematically induce the Law of Gravity by Book III. The *Prin-*

cipia teaches us nothing about the creative process; it is the polished, finished product, and affords no glimpse of the struggle with ideas.[2]

Of course experimental physicists work with students in their laboratories, and artists require privacy for some of their creative efforts. Again the difference between both creative types is not universal; rather, it is one of frequency. Artists are more likely to expose their creative souls, their errors and their frustrations—not just their successes. The likelihood of the art student being treated as a creative colleague rather than a lowly apprentice is simply greater than for the budding literary critic. Sharing stimulates and abets learning. Established academic citizens could improve their students' as well as their own work by borrowing the creative practices of people in the arts.

CREATIVE EFFORTS

Turning to the creative act and the conditions necessary for its realization, artists share many ingredients with their colleagues in the traditional liberal arts. If enumerating and briefly elaborating the basic conditions for creative work seem to indict the university, it is because the university too easily lapses into practices which run counter to her goal as a discoverer of new truths, a creator of beauty, and an analyzer of proper actions. As new inhabitants, artists can remind the university how to function properly and effectively. They also can teach her to try some alternate methods for better achieving her ends. But artists can also learn from others in the university who have survived and remained productive.

To begin, the old saw that starvation is the mother of invention receives no substantiation. Sound support produces higher-quality work than does a vow of poverty. Artists become more, not less, productive with the facilities and eco-

2. Galileo's *Two New Sciences* and *Two Chief World Systems* give us more clues, but even his dialogues, like Plato's, were written after, not during, the creative process. We could be deceived.

nomic security the university provides. Moonlighting and hustling do not increase their creative output. The geologist's laboratory and the French literature scholar's library collection are corresponding requisites to bringing ideas to fruition. Adequate support is a sine qua non, not the precipitator of sloth.

Freedom, too, is an essential ingredient in the creative life that both printmaker and linguist require—freedom to explore the unknown, freedom to venture into new media or disciplines, and freedom to fail. Composer or mathematician, neither can work under imposed constraints and prescribed outcomes. A dictated solution to a commission violates the artist's absolute need for freedom just as viciously as does the artificial establishment of boundaries within which the psychologist must find the best conditions for learning.

Third, liberal arts professors and fine arts professors call attention to the critical role time plays in the creative process. Large blocks of uncommitted and unscheduled time are seen as requisites for productive work. In addition to extended time intervals, there are cyclical changes and alterations associated with maturing and aging. For example, the microbiologist's intricate experiments in his early years change to works of a larger scope in mid-career and more to philosophical pieces later on. Artists experience a corresponding phenomenon along a time dimension which universities must heed. They too have "dry periods" and the need to explore new media.[3]

Support, freedom, and the control of time, then, are essentials within the creative process and are of as much importance to the long-time resident of the university as they are to the im-

3. Intrinsic satisfaction, competitiveness, internal drive, and other attributes related to creativity are less known and understood with respect to typical productive faculty. We did not probe artists on these factors although occasionally unsolicited remarks were offered. We suspect that here, too, while some differences will appear between the two principal groups of creative individuals, the fundamental creative similarities between the pianist and the physical chemist are greater than the differences. The topic receives attention in another context below, on Donald Pelz's notion of an environment of creative tension.

migrant. The interviews, however, suggest at least one basic difference—almost a paradox. This difference concerns the criteria and the processes by which creativity is judged.

First, the paradox. Artists create "products" whose criteria for excellence are the least formally (i.e., verbally) prescribed and agreed upon. At the same time, a developing musician need play but a single passage and his teacher can be fairly sure about his chance ever to reach the top. In the humanities and sciences, on the other hand, and particularly in the quantitative disciplines, few dispute degrees of quality. In these disciplines, however, professors' predictions about the future creative success of their students have not been outstanding. What puzzles the astronomy professor is the large number of his potential stars who never orbit. Brilliance as a student doesn't predict very well a future place in the firmament of outstanding scientists.

As for what the natives can teach the recent arrivals, and vice versa, we note those items which have the greatest potential consequences. For example, some artists believe an unhealthy emotional state exists among their colleagues who lack national and international reputations. With some very visible exceptions (ones which no doubt precipitate artists' erroneous inferences), artists' less visible peers are happy contributors to students, the university, and society. Just as liberal arts departments have their luminary or two, so too are they predominantly populated with less famous faculty who are nonetheless creative individuals, excellent pedagogues, held in high esteem by students, and, overall, happy people. Perhaps envy or jealousy surface from time to time. Even then, however, most likely the jealousy is less intense within a given college than between the superstars across the country competing between themselves for recognition as *the* leading artist of the universe.[4]

4. Two matters enter here and need to be kept distinct. As George M. Foster advances in his "Anatomy of Envy: A Story in Symbolic Behavior" (*Current Anthropology*, 13 [Apr., 1972], 165–202), fear of envy is a pan-phenomenon and by no means absent from academic circles. When relations are expected to be collegial and coequal but are not, the advantaged fear the envy of all others and act to diffuse it. For example, artists of national reputation do more than their

Second, as noted above, a good communication network exists within the established disciplines. Biomedical researchers need no one single university for stimulation and critique, but artists claim they require New York City. Perhaps the differences between academics and artists reside in the nature of the created work. Indeed, a photograph of a painting is a poor substitute for the original, and even an excellent recording is not a live performance. But music scores are transportable, and so are artists and their works, much more easily today than yesterday, although they still cannot reach the universal audience scholarly journals can. What New York really has, then, is not only a critical mass of creators but (just as important) a sufficient collection of critics. Not all universities have such collections of experts as yet, but artistic communities are growing as universities become cities unto themselves and as a variety of artists take up residence in these island paradises. So one of the problems of the creative process is solving itself with the passing of time.

Finally, the settlers might observe the old-timer's skill in the cooperative creative act. Indeed, the philosophical scholar is as alone as is the sculptor: creativity is not the outcome of a committee meeting. However, the recent joint research from mixed scientific specialists has been judged extraordinarily successful. Collaboration among musicians, dancers, and visual artists on multi-media presentations is still a fairly rare occurrence, but artists might take more clues from their neighbors around the campus.

And what can the patriarchs learn from the recent arrivals? Some very important things, as a matter of fact.

share when on campus. Also, they will avoid pain by selecting their closest friends outside their immediate competitors within their university. Outside, however, and this is the second aspect, competition between outstanding artists can be fierce but it lacks envy, for then the contest is between equals.

Creative outlets for the two professorial groups is discussed extensively below in the section on the physical and human work environment. Bringing ideas to fruition remains a salient topic, perhaps the single most important contribution this analysis uncovers.

While the standard disciplines have been wrestling with charges that elitism is the equivalent of racism, sexism, and agism, with egalitarianism versus meritocracy, and with quotas and goals for this, that, and everything else, the arts have never confused creative excellence with secondary attributes. Artists indulge in endless debates on quality, indeed, but never on the basis of non-professional criteria. At the same time, the arts have not received criticism regarding access that the long-standing landholders of academe have wrestled with of late.

Concerning excellence and criteria, artists seem far more introspective than are the more established residents. They have looked back, around, and ahead. They know where they have been, what they are currently about, and what and where they believe they will explore next. Certainly traditional scholars exercise these same psychological analyses, particularly with respect to the present.[5] But it seems highly unlikely that they assess their strengths and weaknesses as thoroughly and candidly as artist-professors. Perhaps such introspection is nothing more than a natural phenomenon new enclaves engage in. If so, academics only need be reminded of the virtues of the practice. Sorting means from ends, clarifying aspirations, recognizing limitations and strengths, setting in balance the short- from the long-range goal—these are healthy activities for academics too.

Finally, artists display a willingness to try something new "for the fun of it." In these days of institutional non-growth, concerns for sparking innovations, and the trends toward self-serving ends when uncertainties regarding the future increase, universities desperately need individuals whose exploratory spirit is high. It is to be hoped that artists' pioneering attitudes will be contagious.

So each constituency can gain by borrowing from the other, permanently and at no cost. Creativity is more than personal, as we have seen. For the creative process to be maintained and

5. We have no similar records of academic scholars on this topic, a genuine need.

improved, there must be a creative response from competent colleagues, a social phenomenon. Hence we turn next to the environment in which creative people work, in particular the human portion of the work climate.

THE WORK ENVIRONMENT

Environmental requisites to support creative faculty differ little between the composer and the geneticist. Both need colleagueship as well as privacy.[6] As Pelz has demonstrated,[7] both produce best when creative tension is high, that is, when support is adequate (but not so great as to induce complacency) and challenge is present. Given individuals with sufficient competence, creative tension results from the proper balance of challenge and security. Challenge comes from both a personal curiosity and the environment's exposing people to new problems. Security derives from the personal attributes of flexibility and self-confidence, although of course the organization can build and destroy self-confidence. (That is, self-confidence sometimes is the *cause* of the necessary security for creative tension, other times the *effect*.) Moreover, the institution controls other factors needed for adequate security—resources, opportunities to engage in problem-solving, and means for rewarding and/or bestowing recognition on the creative individual.

There are some environmental differences, of course. Some liberal arts faculty assume and enjoy administrative roles as careers progress—the management of research projects, the launching of institutes and centers, the political activity of the academic senate. The university needs such participants and rewards those who gravitate to such activities. Artists show less inclination for these career alterations, quite possibly because

6. Neither prefers to engage in departmental political contests but both will do so when the stakes are high—when there is to be a decision affecting their work environment, for example.

7. Donald C. Pelz, "Creative Tensions in the Research and Development Climate," *Science*, 157 (July, 1967), 160–65.

the university has provided galleries and auditoriums for the display of their creative efforts. In this one uncomplicated way, by providing for greater exposure and critique of faculty creative effort, the university community can learn a tactic it needs to know.

As Storer has described so persuasively,[8] the creative act aborts if there is no creative response. That is, unless an effort (idea, production, problem solution, etc.) is critiqued by qualified peers, the creative act exists purely as therapy. Unviewed paintings, unheard sonatas, and unread poems fail to fulfill the criteria of the creative act, for creativity has a social dimension. Without professional judgment there is no way the creative individual can deepen his understanding and skills and move to an even higher level of performance. New growth requires a creative response, and the creative response requires a medium of exchange, a marketplace for the appropriate display of creation.

Of course the scholarly journals serve this function in the traditional academic disciplines. An anonymous editorial board mercilessly desecrates submitted articles, providing a first-level creative response. Those pieces reaching publication have an international audience of critics, providing grist for the next creative effort.

Well and good for a fortunate few, but the protocol is devastating for many. Journals reject manuscripts at rates approaching 90 percent in some disciplines, and the total distribution outlet is but a fraction of what the potential contributors could turn out. For example, if every member of the American Historical Association had but one creative idea in his thirty-five-year tenure in his college, the odds are still small that a major effort would be published. The space simply is not there.

Now of course the competitive process acts as a fine sieve for sorting out the very best, and that is no minor service. Information overload generates specialization and subspecialization,

8. Norman W. Storer, *The Social System of Science* (New York: Holt, 1966).

knowledge of more and more about less and less approaching the limit of absolute minutiae. What is amiss, however, is the "all-or-none" nature of the current structure and communication exchange process. That some outstanding creations never become visible is inevitable in the human process just described, and that is a serious flaw.

Equally serious, however, and perhaps even more so, is the stultifying effect limited access has on so many able and competent human beings. The recognition or reward for faculty creative effort is typically nonexistent as matters now stand. More often it is even negative. Defeat and failure set in. Self-confidence fails. Probably even curiosity wanes. The eager and excited novitiate confronts failure after failure and turns to reordering his values and priorities in order to live with himself. "I'll be a teacher," he says. "Teaching is what is really important in college. Most scholarship is trivia. The journals already are filled with 98 percent trash." His rationalizations select dictums which possess fair degrees of truth, albeit irrelevant truth.

But painters do not stop their creative work because an entry fails to win a prize. Pianists do not stop playing when an invitation from Orchestra Hall fails to arrive. Sculptors do not set down their tools when a critic pans their show—at least not forever.

The behavior differences between historians and printmakers stem from complex causes. However, one simple practice accounts for a critical factor. The university has an orchestra which may play a composer's music even if the Boston Symphony has turned it down. The university has a gallery for an art show even if the Museum of Modern Art did not select the canvas. In short, while the audience may not contain the same size and degree of expertise, a creative response is given and the artist can go on to new work. He can receive response away from home, too, in art fairs and in less renowned concert halls. His is not an all-or-none enterprise. He will not put his easel in the attic and turn to "teaching art" if he lacks the reputation of a Picasso.

The old saw of "he who cannot, teaches" not only pains; it cuts off creativity and sullies an honorable calling at the same time that it weakens that calling's very essence—enhancing creativity.

Colleges and universities also need forums for professors of Romance literature and anthropology. They need techniques and devices for recognizing creative acts. Educational Testing Service, for example, has a practice worth heeding. Naturally a project they undertake requires a report, and assessment of a kind appropriate to the problem under attack. The investigators must then get two favorable reviews from their own staff. Then the manuscript becomes a mimeographed publication for circulation within-house, a device which recognizes the effort and which also permits a creative response. Some papers go no further (like the local art show) whereas others undergo revision once again and move out to the larger audience of critics across the globe, to the appropriate scholarly journals.

Other models come to mind and need not be elaborated upon here. What matters is that artists can teach the university a great deal about creativity and productivity. The university will be better when it learns from its new inhabitants how faculty remain productive.

What can artists learn from the original university settlers? Probably not as much. Liberal arts faculty apparently do not trust administrators the way artists do. While this may reflect an unfounded professorial paranoia, no doubt its historical antecedents gave good cause for faculty demands to participate in decision-making. The lesson, we suppose, is that artists maintain a respectful wariness as they remain withdrawn from the university political arena.

There is a second little piece of advice long-standing residents might pass on. While some colleges may revere their faculty and even express affection on an occasion or two, universities do not love their professors. Reward them, yes, and share in the acclaim they bring, but "love," no. Universities neither possess nor give. So the artist had best not have unfulfillable hopes shattered if institutional love is important to him.

Third, both liberal and fine arts faculties know that wise administrators will leave creative persons alone. Here they can support and reinforce one another, for administrators are known to lose their wisdom on some occasions.

Fourth, fine and liberal arts people alike can learn that if they are called to administrative roles, they will be healthier and better in their job if they take some creative work with them, even if the energy they expend is more directed toward completing creative ideas than it is in generating fresh ones.

And, of course, the old and the new will reinforce the drive for excellence, the need for protection from unfounded and irrelevant attacks from without, and the enhancement and enrichment of truth, beauty, and goodness.

In balance, then, while the newly moved-in artist faculty can learn from, support, and be supported by the long-time residents, actually they can teach the old-timers some highly important matters regarding the creative life. This is a happy and unanticipated outcome of a union both sides resisted for a good many years. Now when playwrights and actors and dancers and novelists and poets make their permanent home in the university in the next few years, the transition will be less traumatic and the prediction of a flourishing community can be made with much greater confidence. Everyone will benefit when the university improves its creative productivity.

Bibliography

"The Arts and the University," *Universities Quarterly*, 10 (Feb., 1956), entire issue.

Baumol, William J., and William G. Bowen. *Performing Arts—the Economic Dilemma*. New York: Twentieth Century Fund, 1966.

Brandstadter, J. T. "The Artist in Higher Education," *Art Journal*, 29 (Fall, 1969), 45, 104.

Brewer, Joseph. "The Creative Artist in the College Community," *Association of American Colleges Bulletin*, 27 (May, 1941), 255–60.

Clapp, Philip G. "The Place of the State University in the American Scheme of Musical Education," *Music Teachers National Association Proceedings* (Detroit, 1921), 57–63.

Clarke, Eric T. "Can Music Teachers Be Artists and Educators?" *Music Teachers National Association Proceedings* (Pittsburgh, 1939), 24–30.

Conant, Howard. "On the Education of Artists," *Art Journal*, 24 (Spring, 1965), 240–43.

Cone, Edward T. "The Creative Artist in the University," *American Scholar*, 16 (Apr., 1947), 192–200.

Council on Higher Education in the American Republics. *The Arts and the University*. New York: Institute of International Education, 1964.

Dennis, Lawrence E., and Renata M. Jacob, eds. *The Arts in Higher Education*. San Francisco: Jossey-Bass, 1968.

Dickinson, Edward. *Music and the Higher Education*. New York: Scribner's, 1915.

Dolph, Jack. "Teacher or Performer . . . Which?" *Music Journal*, 16 (Jan., 1958), 84, 95.

Dunham, Rowland W. "The Musician and the Doctor's Degree," *AAUP Bulletin*, 34 (June, 1948), 375–81.

Durst, D. "Artists and College Art Teaching," *College Art Journal*, 16 (Spring, 1957), 222–29.

Epperson, Gordon. "University Music: Theoretical or Applied?" *AAUP Bulletin*, 44 (Summer, 1958), 616–21.

Falls, Gregory A. "New Leadership Roles for the University in the Arts," *Arts in Society*, 3, no. 2 (1966), 295–97.

Finney, Ross Lee. "Can a College Professor Compose?" *Music Journal*, 17 (June–July, 1959), 18, 54–55.

Finney, Theodore M. "The American College and University as a
Center of Musical Activity," *Music Teachers National Association Proceedings* (San Francisco, 1911), 803–6.

Franzen, Bengt. "The Professional Musician and the Music Educator,"
Music Educators Journal, 41 (Nov.–Dec., 1954), 34–36.

Goldman, Freda H. *The Arts in Higher Adult Education*. Brookline,
Mass.: Center for the Study of Liberal Education for Adults, Boston
University, 1966.

Grout, Donald J. "The Divorce of Music and Learning," in *Perspectives
in Music Education, Source Book III*, ed. Bonnie C. Kowall. Washington, D.C.: Music Educators National Conference, 1966.

Herstaud, Arnold L. "The Environment of the Artist on the Small College Campus," *Art Journal*, 21 (Spring, 1962), 164–66.

Howe, Richard. "Great Teacher-Performer Conflict," *Music Journal*, 20
(Oct., 1962), 32–33.

Kennedy, James P. "The Concert Artist in Education," *Music Journal*,
25 (Mar., 1967), 87–88.

Kinkeldey, Otto. "The Artist and the Scholar," *Music Teachers National
Association Proceedings* (Pittsburgh, 1940), 67–79.

Kohs, Ellis B. "Status of the Composer-Educator," *Musical America*, 70
(Sept., 1950), 29.

Leepa, A. "Role of the Professional Artist in Colleges and Universities," *College Art Journal*, 19 (Winter, 1959–60), 166–68.

Lehman, Paul R. "The Performer and the Doctorate," *American Music
Teacher*, 14 (Mar.–Apr., 1965), 17, 40.

Lippman, Joseph A. "Dear Concert Artist: Your Life Is Not Your
Own," *Music Journal*, 20 (Nov.–Dec., 1962), 58, 69, 91, 94.

Lowry, W. McNeil. "The Arts," in *The Contemporary University:
U.S.A.*, ed. Robert S. Morison. Boston: Houghton-Mifflin, 1966.

———. "The University and the Creative Arts," *Arts in Society*, 2, no. 3
(1963), 7–21.

Mahoney, Margaret, ed. *The Arts on Campus: The Necessity for Change*.
Greenwich, Conn.: New York Graphic Society, 1970.

Meredith, William. "The Artist as Teacher, the Poet as Troublemaker,"
Harvard Educational Review, 36 (Fall, 1966), 518–22.

Mitchell, Ronald E. "Encouraging the Arts in the University," *Arts in
Society*, 3, no. 1 (1966), 32–39.

Morgan, P. "The Role of Artist-in-Residence in a School or College,"
College Art Journal, 7 (Spring, 1948), 168–71.

Morrison, Jack. *The Rise of the Arts on the American Campus*. New York: McGraw-Hill, 1973.

Pepper, Stephen C. "How to Fit Universities for Artists," *American Scholar*, 9 (Spring, 1940), 192–200.

Perkins, James A. "Should the Artist Come to the Campus?" *Saturday Review*, July 17, 1965, 54–56.

———. "The University and the Arts," *Teachers College Record*, 66 (May, 1965), 671–78.

Pleasants, Henry. "Crescendo on the Campus: Our New Music Centers," *The Reporter*, Sept., 1965, 52–56.

"Poets as Dons," *Universities Quarterly*, 13 (Aug./Oct., 1959), entire issue.

Ratcliffe, Hardie. "The Social and Economic Position of the Performing Musician," *National Music Council Bulletin*, 22 (Winter, 1961–62), 11–12.

Read, Gardner. "Artist-in-Residence: Fact or Fancy?" *Arts in Society*, 3 (Summer, 1966), 478–83.

Rickey, George. "Arts Program of the Association of American Colleges," *Association of American Colleges Bulletin*, 34 (Oct., 1948), 295–99.

Risenhoover, Morris. "Artist-Teachers in Universities: Studies in Role Integration." Ph.D. dissertation, University of Michigan, 1972.

Ritchie, Andrew. *The Visual Arts in Higher Education*. New Haven: College Art Association, 1966.

Rockefeller Panel (reporting on the future of theater, dance, and music in America). *The Performing Arts: Problems and Prospects*. New York: McGraw-Hill, 1965.

Rosenberg, Bernard, and Morris E. Fliegel. *The Vanguard Artist*. New York: Quadrangle Press, 1965.

Rosenberg, Harold. "The Art Establishment," *Esquire*, 62 (Jan., 1965), 43–46, 114.

———. "Problems in the Teaching of Artists," *Art Journal*, 24 (Winter, 1964–65), 135–38.

Roy, Vincent. "The Free Lance Artist as a Teacher of Art," in *Art in American Life and Education*, Fortieth Yearbook of the National Society for the Study of Education. Bloomington, Ind.: Public School Publishing Co., 1941.

Schulze, F. "Role of the Artist-in-Residence in a Small Liberal Arts College," *College Art Journal*, 19 (Summer, 1960), 353–55.

Schwartz, Will. "Universities: Guardians of Our Musical Heritage,"
    Music Educators Journal, 47 (Sept.–Oct., 1960), 41–43.
Skinner, Robert G. "Perceptions of Some Artists in Residence in Ohio
    Colleges and Universities." Ph.D. dissertation, Ohio University,
    1971.
Sloane, J. D. "The Scholar and the Artist," *Art Journal,* 23 (Fall, 1963),
    16–19.
Smith, D. L. "Great Artists as Art Teachers," *American Artist,* 29 (Sept.,
    1965), 58–63.
Smith, Russell F. W. "A Community of Artists and Scholars," *Arts in
    Society,* 2, no. 3 (1963), 66–74.
Smith, Warren S. "The Artist in the Community of Scholars," *AAUP
    Bulletin,* 45 (June, 1959), 237–42.
Super, Sister Dolores. "Musical Performance in American Higher Edu-
    cation 1850–1951." Ed.D. dissertation, University of Michigan, 1970.
Swinton, G. "The Artist and the University Community," *College Art
    Journal,* 18 (Winter, 1959), 144–48.
Thompson, Randall. *College Music: An Investigation for the Association
    of American Colleges.* New York: Macmillan, 1935.
Treger, Charles. "The Artist in the University," *Music Journal,* 23 (May,
    1965), 29.
"The University as Cultural Leader," *Arts in Society,* 3, no. 4 (1966), en-
    tire issue.
Wald, George. "The Artist in the University," *Arts in Society,* 2, no. 3
    (1963), 59–65.
Watrous, James. "Universities and the Visual Arts," *Art Journal,* 23
    (Fall, 1963), 1, 58–60.
Wickiser, R. L. "The Artist as a Teacher," *College Art Journal,* 11 (Win-
    ter, 1951), 121–22.
Winslow, Leon. "Artists in Residence in Colleges," in *Art in American
    Life and Education,* Fortieth Yearbook of the National Society for the
    Study of Education. Bloomington, Ind.: Public School Publishing
    Co., 1941.
Yont, Rose. *Status and Value of Music in Education.* Lincoln, Neb.:
    Woodruff Press, 1916.